Western Region

STOKES
Beginner's Guide
to Birds

W9-BRM-245

Donald and Lillian Stokes

Little, Brown and Company

New York Boston

Little, Brown and Company
Time Warner Book Group
1271 Avenue of the Americas, New York, NY 10020
Visit our Web site at www.twbookmark.com

First Edition

10 9 8

TWP

Library of Congress Cataloging-in-Publication Data

Stokes, Donald W.
     Stokes beginner's guide to birds, Western
     region / Donald and Lillian Stokes. —
     1st ed.
        p.   cm.
     Includes index.
     ISBN 0-316-81812-7
     1. Birds — West (U.S.) — Identification.
I. Stokes, Lillian Q. II. Title.
QL683.W4S756   1996
598.2978 — dc20   96-13003

Designed by Barbara Werden

Printed in Singapore

Color Tab Index

Birds are grouped by color. Within a color group they are arranged roughly by size, from the smallest to the largest.

Birds with large amounts of yellow

Birds that have black or slate-gray and orange

Birds that are mostly red

Birds that are mostly brown

Birds with large amounts of blue

Birds with any green

Birds that are all white

Birds that are mostly black

Birds that are mostly black and white

Birds that are red, black, and white

Birds that are mostly gray

Stokes Field Guides

Stokes Field Guide to Birds: Eastern Region

Stokes Field Guide to Birds: Western Region

Stokes Field Guide to Bird Songs: Eastern Region (CD/cassette)

Stokes Field Guide to Bird Songs: Western Region (CD/cassette)

Stokes Beginner's Guides

Stokes Beginner's Guide to Bats

Stokes Beginner's Guide to Birds: Eastern Region

Stokes Beginner's Guide to Birds: Western Region

Stokes Beginner's Guide to Butterflies

Stokes Beginner's Guide to Dragonflies

Stokes Beginner's Guide to Shorebirds

Stokes Backyard Nature Books

Stokes Bird Feeder Book

Stokes Bird Gardening Book

Stokes Birdhouse Book

Stokes Bluebird Book

Stokes Butterfly Book

Stokes Hummingbird Book

Stokes Oriole Book

Stokes Purple Martin Book

Stokes Wildflower Book: East of the Rockies

Stokes Wildflower Book: From the Rockies West

Stokes Nature Guides

Stokes Guide to Amphibians and Reptiles

Stokes Guide to Animal Tracking and Behavior

Stokes Guide to Bird Behavior, Volume 1

Stokes Guide to Bird Behavior, Volume 2

Stokes Guide to Bird Behavior, Volume 3

Stokes Guide to Enjoying Wildflowers

Stokes Guide to Nature in Winter

Stokes Guide to Observing Insect Lives

Other Stokes Books

The Natural History of Wild Shrubs and Vines

Contents

How to Use This Guide

Stokes Beginner's Guide to Birds: Western Region includes 100 of the species you are most likely to see when you first start to watch birds. Below is a description of the main parts of the guide and how to use them.

Alphabetical Index

Inside the front and back covers is the alphabetical index. This helps you look up a species you are already familiar with but about which you want more information. The birds are arranged in alphabetical order by their last names. Thus, American Robin is listed under *R* for Robin, Western Gull is listed under *G* for Gull.

Color Tab Index

The Color Tab Index makes it easy to look up birds.

When you see a bird, determine its main color and use the tab with that color to get you to the right section of the guide. Once there, look among the birds for the one that looks most like the bird you have seen. People see colors differently, so if you do not find your bird in your first choice of color tab, try the color that would be your second-best guess. The birds in each section are arranged roughly by size, with the smaller at the start and the larger at the end.

When male and female of a species are different colors, they are shown under different color tabs with a small photograph of the opposite sex inserted in the corner of the main photograph to show that they are the same species.

Identification Pages

Each species identification account starts with the bird's common name in large letters, followed by its scientific name in smaller italic letters. Then the length of the bird is given, measured from the tip of its bill to the tip of its tail. Each species account also includes the following:

I.D. — This section points out the main features of the bird that distinguish it from other species.

In some species, the male and

female look different; in other species, the birds have different plumage in summer and winter. In these cases, you will see the headings MALE, FEMALE, SUMMER, WINTER before the descriptions of the different plumages.

For some species you will see an immature plumage. This is marked in the text by the word IMMATURE and refers to any plumage of a young bird (from its first winter on) that is unlike that of the adult. In some species, such as gulls, young birds take up to 4 years to look like the adults.

For a few species we show the juvenal plumage. This is the plumage worn in the first summer. It is marked by the word JUVENILE.

Voice — This is a description of the main sounds that you may hear the bird make. Knowing these sounds can help you identify birds and also introduce you to their language. Many of our smaller birds give *songs;* these are complex sounds that are partly instinctive and partly learned. In many species, only the male sings. All other vocal sounds birds make are called *calls;* these are usually short, simple sounds that are instinctively given without any previous learning.

Habitat — This describes the areas with their types of plants where you are most likely to find the bird. Each species has its own habitat needs. For example, for nesting, meadowlarks need fields, nuthatches need woods, and mockingbirds need shrubs. Without these habitats, these birds cannot survive. This is why preserving habitats is so important to conserving birds.

This section also shows what has happened to the population of this species from 1966 to 1993. This information is given next to the word POPULATION. It is based on a North American census called the Breeding Bird Survey, in which volunteers go out on a fixed route each year at approximately the same time and count all breeding birds.

If the population has risen less than 40% over the 27-year period, there is a single arrow up (↑); if the population has risen over 40%, there is a double arrow up (⇑). If the population has fallen less than 40%, there is a single arrow down (↓); if the population has fallen more than 40%, there is a double arrow down (⇓).

Things that cause bird populations to decline include loss of nesting or feeding habitat, disease, harsh weather, and pollution. Things that allow bird populations to increase include new feeding or breeding habitat, favorable weather, and spreading out to live in a larger geographical range.

Becoming aware of the population trends of birds is a good way to see which species are in trouble and need our attention and help to survive.

Nesting — Here you will learn all about the fascinating nesting habits of birds. Not only are these interesting to know, they may also help you understand a bird's behavior as you watch it during the breeding period.

First there is a description of the materials and placement of the nest.

Following this are details of the nesting cycle, with letters used to indicate each part of the cycle. These include:

EGGS = The average number of eggs and their color.
I = The number of days spent *incubating* the eggs; this is the time when generally just the female sits over the eggs to warm them so that the chicks can develop inside.
N = The time that the hatched young remain in the nest, called the *nestling phase*. If there is no N, then the young leave the nest upon hatching.
F = The time from when the eggs hatch to when the young can first fly, a moment called *fledging*.
B = The number of times per year

an individual bird is likely to go through a complete nesting cycle, or *brood*.

Attracting — This section indicates what you can do to help provide for a bird's feeding and nesting needs. There are sections on bird feeders and which seeds are favored, birdhouses and their correct dimensions, and any plantings you can add to make your yard a more attractive habitat for that species. Bird feeder, birdhouse, and birdbath symbols quickly point out which species use them.

Dimensions for birdhouses include the diameter of the entrance hole and the distance between the bottom of the hole and the floor of the house. We also mention the size of the floor area.

Range Map — This map gives you a good idea of where a bird lives in summer and winter.

Yellow = Summer range
Green = Year-round range
Blue = Winter range

Use the range maps to help you know if a bird is likely to occur in your area in a particular season. When you are trying to identify a bird, range maps can also help you eliminate certain species from consideration by showing that they do not live in your area.

If the range map for a bird shows only a yellow summer range, this means that the species migrates south for the winter, usually to Central or South America, both of which are outside the area of the map.

Tips on Identifying Birds

Identifying birds is a wonderful challenge and can develop into an exciting skill and hobby that you can enjoy all of your life.

What follows are a few tips for the beginner on how to more successfully identify the birds you see:

1. Describe before you identify. Notice and describe what you see to yourself and try to memorize this before you look up the bird. What colors do you see? Where are the colors on the bird? Where is the bird — on the ground, at a feeder, near water? What is the bird doing — pecking at bark, eating a seed, creeping down a tree?

2. Use the photographs as guidelines for identification. Within a species, individuals vary; some may be slightly darker, some may be slightly larger, some may have slightly longer bills. Even the same individual bird can look different; in cold weather birds will often puff out their feathers to stay warm and in warm weather they may sleek their feathers to cool off.

3. If possible, get binoculars so that you can see birds up close.

When you have learned most of the birds in this guide, go get our more complete field guide, *Stokes Field Guide to Birds: Eastern Region* or *Western Region*.

Attracting Birds

There are four main ways that you can attract more birds to your property: bird feeders, birdhouses, birdbaths, and plantings.

Setting Up Bird Feeders

Feeding birds is a wonderful way to increase the number of birds around your house and to see them up close. Over 65 million people in the United States feed birds in their backyards, and there is a good reason why this is such a popular hobby — it is great fun, it helps the birds, it reduces stress, and it brings you closer to nature.

You can enjoy feeding birds all year; in fact, in some cases you may attract more birds in spring through fall than you will in winter. This is because more species are here in summer than in winter.

There are many kinds of bird feeders: some for seed, some for suet, and others for sugar solutions. Here is a brief description of each type and how to use it:

Seed Feeders — Some feeders are designed for just thistle seed. They are usually tubular, with tiny openings just big enough for the thistle seed. They attract goldfinches, House Finches, Pine Siskins, chickadees, and others.

The vast majority of seed feeders take other types of seed. They may be tubular with perches, or like a small hopper with a platform underneath. Although any kind of seed can be put in these feeders, most birds that come to them prefer just sunflower seed, or a mixed seed with a high proportion of sunflower seed.

Seed feeders can be hung or mounted on a pole. In either case, place them 8 ft. from the nearest place from which a squirrel could jump, and try to get a baffle — a disklike shield placed above or below a feeder — to help keep the squirrels off. Birds that regularly come to these types of feeders include chickadees, titmice, nuthatches, House Finches, goldfinches, jays, and others.

You can also scatter seed directly on open ground underneath your other feeders or on a small traylike platform just above the ground. This is good for the many species that prefer to feed on the ground, such as juncos, sparrows, towhees, Mourning Doves, and others. In these situations try sunflower seed, seed mixes, white millet, or cracked corn.

Suet Feeders — Suet is fat from around the kidneys of cattle. You can buy it at your supermarket meat counter, or you can buy suet cakes from your local bird-feeder supply store. Suet cakes are rendered suet that stays solid better in warm weather. They often contain other things birds like, such as peanuts, fruit, or insect parts. Suet cakes usually fit directly into a wire basket that can be nailed to a tree or hung from a seed feeder.

Birds that are attracted to suet include woodpeckers, chickadees, titmice, nuthatches, and jays.

Hummingbird Feeders — Hummingbirds are easy to attract with special feeders that hold a sugar solution.

To make the sugar solution, combine 1 cup sugar (*not* honey) with 4 cups water and boil for 1–2 minutes. Let cool and then place some in the feeder and store the rest in the refrigerator for later use. Do not add red dye to the solution in an attempt to further attract hummingbirds; it is not needed and may harm the birds. Besides, there is usually red on the feeder.

Be sure to replace the solution every 3 days to keep it fresh and free of mold, which might hurt the birds.

Using Birdhouses

In addition to feeders, a great way to attract birds is by putting up birdhouses. They not only provide needed cavities for nesting, but they also enable you to watch a bird throughout its breeding cycle.

Some species of birds typically nest in tree holes, either a natural cavity or one they excavate. These birds often accept human-made houses that imitate their natural nest holes.

About 25 species of birds commonly use birdhouses. These include chickadees, titmice, wrens, bluebirds, Purple Martins, nuthatches, starlings, some flycatchers, some swallows, some owls, and some woodpeckers. The birds in this guide that use birdhouses have a small symbol of a birdhouse under the section on **Attracting.**

Features of a Good Birdhouse — There are many types of birdhouses available for sale. Not all are good for birds. Here are a few things to look for in a good birdhouse:

1. It should have only one entrance hole (except in the case of Purple Martin bird-houses).
2. You should be able to open it, so you can monitor the bird's success through nesting and clean out the nest when the young have fledged.
3. It should be the right dimensions for the species you are trying to attract.
4. It should have ventilation holes at the top and drainage holes in the bottom.
5. It should be made of wood, for this insulates the house from heat and cold.
6. It should not have a perch in front of the hole; the birds do not need it, and it might help predators get inside.
7. The roof should overhang the entrance hole to protect it from sun and rain.
8. There should be a way to mount the box to a post or pole.

These are minimum good features. Any birdhouse without these should not be used.

Where and When to Put Up a Birdhouse — Birdhouses can be placed on poles in the open, on trees, on fence posts, or on the sides of buildings. Some birds will tolerate nesting closer to human activity than others.

Most birdhouses should be placed about 5–6 ft. high. This way you can easily clean them out at the end of the breeding season. It does not matter which compass direction they face.

You can place several birdhouses in different locations on your property and see which ones the birds prefer.

You can put up birdhouses at any time of year, but fall through early spring is the best time, for the birds use them in late spring through summer.

Birdhouse Dimensions — Several dimensions of a birdhouse are critical to the safe and successful breeding of the birds that use it:

Size of the entrance hole — The entrance hole must be large and smooth enough to enable the birds to go in and out without too much wear on their feathers.

Distance from the hole to the floor — The floor must be far enough beneath the entrance hole to allow the bird room to build its nest and also to prevent predators, such as raccoons, from easily reaching in and grabbing the birds.

Interior dimensions of the floor — These must be large enough to accommodate the nest, but not so large that the bird cannot fill the floor area with its nest.

Birdbaths

Water is a major need of birds. They use it for drinking and bathing. If you put out a birdbath, you will not only help the species that you have attracted with feeders, you will also attract other species that do not come to feeders but still love to bathe and drink from birdbaths.

Place a birdbath somewhere near a shrub or tree where the birds can land before coming to the water and where they can dry off and preen after drinking or bathing.

Some people even provide water all winter in colder climates by getting birdbath heaters.

Plantings

You can make your yard more attractive to birds by adding plants that provide food and nesting habitats.

In general, the more varied the plantings in your yard, the more species you are likely to attract. Here are some types of plants you can add and their benefits to the birds:

Evergreens — Plant several evergreen trees together and you will provide shelter for birds in bad weather and at night when they roost. In addition, many species of common birds nest in evergreens, and the cones may attract seed-eating finches in winter.

Shrubs — Areas of shrubs are a favorite habitat for many birds. They provide nesting habitats for species such as mockingbirds and thrashers, roosting spots for sparrows, and seeds and berries for a wide variety of small birds.

Try to plant a variety of
shrubs, some that produce
berries at different seasons.
Grasses and Wildflowers — These
low plants attract insects in
summer and produce seeds
for the winter, and insects
and seeds are important foods
for many common birds. If
you have an area of your
property that you can just let
grow, you will find many
birds attracted to it.

For More Information

For more information on feeders
and attracting birds, see our other
books:

The Bird Feeder Book
The Hummingbird Book
The Complete Birdhouse Book
The Bluebird Book

About Binoculars

Seeing birds up close is a thrilling experience, and binoculars can be a wonderful aid to this. Here are a few tips about binoculars that will help you get a pair that works for you at the right price and the right quality.

Two Important Numbers

All binoculars have 2 basic numbers associated with them, numbers such as 7 x 35 or 8.5 x 42, for example.

The first number refers to the power of the binoculars to magnify an object, by 7 times or by 8.5 times in the examples above. It is best to get binoculars with magnification power somewhere from 7 to 8.5. More powerful than this and you will have trouble holding the image steady as you look through; any less powerful and you will not see the birds closely enough to identify.

The second number refers to the size, in millimeters, of the opening at the far end of the binoculars. The larger the opening, the more light is let through and the clearer you will see the bird. An opening size somewhere between 35 and 42 is good for most purposes.

Size and Weight

One of the mistakes most beginners make is making weight and size their main criteria for choosing binoculars. They choose very light and very small binoculars so that they can easily take them on hikes and in their pockets.

Unfortunately, very light and small binoculars rarely have the power or let in enough light to be good for bird-watching. A good pair of bird-watching binoculars will probably not fit in your pocket and will weigh about 20–28 oz.

Buy binoculars at a store that carries several brands so that you can try all of them out. Get advice from other people who have binoculars and try looking through different pairs.

If you enjoy bird-watching, it is worthwhile investing in good binoculars. They will bring the birds closer for the rest of your life, resulting in a tremendous amount of beauty and joy.

Helping to Save the Birds

The most important step we can take to help save our wonderful variety of beautiful birds today is to save the variety of habitats in which they live. If you take the home away from humans, they have trouble surviving. The same is true of birds; the habitats in which they live are their homes.

Ten Ways You Can Help Save Birds

Here are a few actions you can take that will help save birds:

1. Learn to identify more birds.
2. Learn more about bird behavior.
3. Learn the population trends of the birds you see.
4. Create good bird habitats in your own backyard by providing bird feeders, birdhouses, birdbaths, and plantings that attract birds.
5. Keep a notebook of your observations.
6. Share your love for and knowledge of birds with others, both young and old.
7. Participate in bird censuses and surveys.
8. Join birding organizations and bird clubs in your area.
9. Join local, national, and international conservation organizations.
10. Help your local conservation commission acquire and manage town lands so that they support more bird life.

Photo Credits

The letter or letters immediately following each page number refer to the position of the photograph on the page (T = top; B = bottom; L = left; R = right; i = a smaller picture inset within the main picture).

Steve Bentsen: 3L, 38, 40, 42, 52.
Rick and Nora Bowers: 11, 24, 33, 44.
Kathleen and Lindsey Brown: 4L, 4R, 31R, 56i, 81L, 81R, 104.
Rob Curtis: 35, 64, 66, 66i, 91, 97.
Mike Danzenbaker: 3R, 8, 19, 32, 39, 45i, 62, 69L, 86, 94R, 106, 107, 115L, 119iT.
Larry Ditto: 58, 74.
Steven D. Faccio: 21.
Kenneth Fink: 14, 71, 83, 94L, 117iT, 117iB, 119iB.
Sam Fried: 10.

Gary Froehlich: 49L, 61i, 87, 110, 116iL, 116iR.
Kevin T. Karlson: 59.
Maslowski Photograph: 6R, 28BR, 34, 96.
Anthony Mercieca: 50, 53R, 68, 75.
Arthur Morris, Birds as Art: 30, 87i, 117.
Photo/Nats: M. Clay — 73R; B. Magnuson — 65L.
Brian Small: 7L, 7R, 12, 15, 16, 20, 23, 37, 41, 46, 47, 70R, 73L, 79, 80, 89, 90, 93, 99, 102, 108, 111.
Hugh P. Smith, Jr.: 9, 17, 22, 25, 28L, 34i, 43, 48, 55i, 65R, 70L, 72L, 72R, 95, 98, 103, 112.
Lillian Stokes: 26, 60, 61, 63, 76, 77, 77i, 78, 85, 86i, 88, 92, 109, 116, 118, 118iT, 118iB, 120.
John Tveten: 82, 84, 113R, 119.

Tom Vezo: 54, 64i, 105.
VIREO: R. and N. Bowers — 69R; W. Greene — 8i, 100; S. Holt — 67; M. P. Kahl — 49R; A. Morris — 31L, 33i; O. S. Pettingill, Jr. — 18; F. K. Schleicher — 115R; J. Schumache — 36; H. P. Smith, Jr. — 51, 114; T. J. Ulrich — 27, 29, 99; R. Villani — 28TR; A. Walther — 101; D. Wechsler — 13L; B. K. Wheeler — 45, 56; D. and M. Zimmerman — 13, 53L.
Brian K. Wheeler: 55.
Art Wolfe: 57.

Identification

Voice

Habitat

Nesting

Birdbath

Bird feeder

Birdhouse

Identification Pages

Lesser Goldfinch
Carduelis psaltria 4¹/₂"

I.D.
MALE: Yellow belly; white patch on wings. In western half of range has black cap and green back. In eastern half of range is all black above. **FEMALE:** Greenish above; yellow below; black wings have a white patch that is seen when the bird flies.

Voice
Song is a rapid series of repeated phrases from other birds' songs; call is a "peeyeet."

Habitat
Woods edges, roadsides, gardens, parks. **POPULATION:** ↓

Nesting
Nest of bark and moss lined with downy materials, placed in shrub or tree. Eggs: 3–6, bluish white; I: 12 days; F: unknown; B: 1 or possibly more.

Attracting

Comes to bird feeders for sunflower and thistle seed.

Male

Female

Tip **In winter, look for it in small flocks, sometimes with other species of goldfinches.**

Comes to birdbaths for drinking and bathing.

3

American Goldfinch
Carduelis tristis 5"

I.D.
SUMMER: Yellow body; black wings and tail. **MALE:** Black cap. **FEMALE:** All-yellow head.

Voice
Flight call is "perchicoree perchicoree"; song is a long canary-like warble or a short forceful warble.

Habitat
Open areas with shrubs and trees, farms, suburban yards, gardens. **POPULATION:** ↓

Nesting
Nest of weed bark fastened with caterpillar webbing, placed in shrub or tree. Eggs: 3–7, light blue; I: 12–14 days; F: 11–15 days; B: 1–2.

Attracting

Prefers thistle or hulled sunflower seed in hanging feeders.

Male, summer

Winter, p. 98

Female, summer

Tip Can look like different birds in winter because they change from yellow to mostly grayish brown.

Comes to birdbaths for drinking and bathing.

Common Yellowthroat

Geothlypis trichas 5"

I.D. **MALE:** Yellow throat and upper breast; black mask with a grayish-white border.

Voice Song sounds like "your money, your money, your money"; phrase goes with the robberlike mask of the male. Call is a sharp "tchet."

Habitat Dense brushy habitats near wet areas; also drier habitats with dense understory. **POPULATION:** ↓

Nesting Cuplike nest of grasses, leaves, and hair, placed in shrubbery. Eggs: 3–4, creamy white with brown marks; I: 12 days; F: 8–9 days; B: 1–2.

Attracting
Planting shrubs near a lake or pond may attract them to nest.

Female, p. 20
Male

Tip If you get near their nest, the birds will approach and give their "tchet" call.

5

Yellow Warbler

Dendroica petechia 5"

I.D.

MALE: Yellow with reddish streaks on breast. **FEMALE:** Paler yellow, with breast streaks fainter or absent.

Voice

Song sounds like "sweet sweet sweet, I'm so sweet"; call is a musical "chip."

Habitat

Shrubby areas, especially near water with willows and alder; also yards, gardens.
POPULATION: ↑

Nesting

Nest of milkweed stem fibers, grasses, and down, placed in an upright fork of shrub or small tree. Eggs: 4–6, white with blotches; I: 10 days; F: 9–11 days; B: 1.

Attracting

Planting shrubs near a lake or pond may attract Yellow Warblers to nest.

Male

Female

Tip Watch for females collecting downy fibers and webbing from tent caterpillar nests to build nests; listen for males singing from exposed perches.

6

Western Tanager

Piranga ludoviciana 7"

I.D.

MALE: Red face; yellow belly; black back, wings, and tail; upper wing bar broad and yellow. **FEMALE:** Greenish yellow; gray back; brown wings with 2 thin wing bars.

Voice

Song is a series of 2- to 3-syllable slow phrases; call is a slurred "pit-er-ic."

Habitat

Coniferous or mixed forests. **POPULATION:** ↑

Nesting

Nest of twigs and rootlets, placed on outer limbs of tree. Eggs: 3–5, pale blue with dark marks; I: 13 days; F: 13–15 days; B: 1 or possibly more.

Attracting

May come to feeders for oranges and grapes.

Male

Female

 Tip **The male is one of the most colorful birds of the West; look for the white wing bars on the female.**

Comes to birdbaths for drinking and bathing.

Evening Grosbeak
Coccothraustes vespertinus 8"

I.D.
MALE: Yellow body; black-and-white wings; darker head with a bright yellow eyebrow. **FEMALE:** Brownish gray overall; black-and-white wings; yellow on back of neck.

Voice
Song is a halting warble; call is a ringing "peer" and when given by a flock is reminiscent of sleighbells.

Habitat
Summers in northern woods; winters in open areas with trees and shrubs. **POPULATION:** ⇑

Nesting
Nest of twigs and moss, placed at end of tree branch. Eggs: 2–5, blue or bluish green with dark marks; I: 11–14 days; F: 13–14 days; B: 2.

Attracting
Prefers sunflower seed.

Female

Male

Tip **Evening Grosbeaks are seen mostly in winter, when they move south from their northern range.**

Planting trees such as ash, maple, and tulip poplar provides natural seeds for them to eat.

8

Bullock's Oriole

Icterus bullockii 8¹/₂″

I.D.

FEMALE: Yellowish head and breast; whitish belly; large sharp-pointed bill.

Voice

Song is 4–8 medium-pitched whistled notes; calls include a 2-note "teetoo" and a rapid chatter, like "ch'ch'ch'ch."

Habitat

Deciduous trees near openings, such as parks, gardens, or along roads. **POPULATION:** ↓

Nesting

Nest is a hanging structure woven from plant fibers and suspended from tip of tree branch. Eggs: 4–6, pale bluish white with dark marks; I: 12–14 days; F: 12–14 days; B: 1.

Attracting

Comes to oriole or hummingbird feeders that offer sugar solution; also eats fruit, such as orange halves.

Male, p. 14

Female

Tip **Suspends its nest from the tips of branches that hang over roads, lawns, or streams.**

9

Western Meadowlark

Sturnella neglecta 9"

I.D.

Streaked brown above; striking yellow below; broad black V on breast. **IN FLIGHT:** Note white outer tail feathers as bird flutters then glides.

Voice

Song is a short phrase of low-pitched flutelike notes; call is a low "chup."

Habitat

Meadows and grasslands. **POPULATION:** ↓

Nesting

Nest is a domed structure of grasses, placed in natural or scraped depression in ground among grasses. Eggs: 3–7, white with dark marks; I: 13–15 days; F: 11–12 days; B: 1–2.

Attracting

Meadowlarks are dependent for their breeding on large grassy fields. It is important that these fields not be mowed until the young can fly.

Tip Females stay and nest in field grasses, but males often fly up to top of fence posts or small shrubs to sing.

10

Yellow-headed Blackbird

Xanthocephalus xanthocephalus
9¹/₂"

I.D.
MALE: Bright yellow hood; black body; white patch on wings shows on perched or flying bird.

Voice
Song is short choked notes, interspersed with long buzzes; call is a low "krrt."

Habitat
Summers in marshes; winters in grain fields. **POPULATION:** ⇑

Nesting
Nest of reeds and grass lined with softer materials, placed low in vegetation above water. Eggs: 3–5, pale greenish with dark marks; I: 11–13 days; F: 9–12 days; B: 2.

Male

Female, p. 44

Tip **In summer, look for it in marshes; in winter, look for it among large flocks of other blackbirds, starlings, and cowbirds.**

Black-headed Grosbeak

Pheucticus melanocephalus 8"

I.D.

MALE: Black head; buffy-orange breast and collar; bold white wing markings on black wings. **IN FLIGHT:** Shows yellow "armpits."

Voice

Song is a series of hurried whistles; call is a squeaky "eek."

Habitat

Deciduous forests, thickets, pine woodlands. **POPULATION:** ↑

Nesting

Nest of twigs, rootlets, and flower heads, placed in fork of tree or shrub. Eggs: 2–5, bluish white or greenish white with brown spots; I: 12–13 days; F: 11–12 days; B: 1 or possibly more.

Attracting

Comes to feeders for fruit or sunflower and mixed seed.

Female, p. 37

Male

Tip Look for this species' large conical bill, which it uses to crack open the hulls of seeds.

Spotted Towhee
Pipilo maculatus 8"

Male

I.D.

MALE: Black hood, back, and wings contrast with orange-brown flanks and white belly; white spotting on wings.

Voice

Song is a high trill; calls are "chewink" or "chweee."

Habitat

Open woods with shrub understory. **POPULATION:** ↑

Nesting

Nest of leaves, strips of bark, and grass, placed on or near ground in scratched depression under brush. Eggs: 2–6, creamy with brown spots; I: 12–13 days; F: 10–12 days; B: 1–3.

Female, p. 40

Tip Listen for the rustling sound it makes in underbrush as it jumps backward to pull away leaves and search for seeds.

Attracting

Comes to feeders for mixed seed scattered on ground.

Bullock's Oriole
Icterus bullockii 8½"

I.D. **MALE:** Orange face; black crown; black eyeline; large white wing patch.

Voice Song is 4–8 medium-pitched whistled notes; calls include a 2-note "teetoo" and a rapid chatter, like "ch'ch'ch'ch."

Habitat Deciduous trees near openings, such as parks, gardens, or along roads. **POPULATION:** ↓

Nesting Nest is a hanging structure woven from plant fibers and suspended from tip of tree branch. Eggs: 4–6, pale bluish white with dark marks; I: 12–14 days; F: 12–14 days; B: 1.

Attracting

Comes to oriole or hummingbird feeders that offer sugar solution; also eats fruit such as orange halves.

Female, p. 9

Male

Tip Suspends its nest from the tips of branches that hang over roads, lawns, or streams.

14

Varied Thrush
Ixoreus naevius 9 1/2"

I.D. Dark above; reddish orange below; orange line behind eyes; 2 orange wing bars. **MALE:** Blue-gray upperparts; broad black breastband. **FEMALE:** Dark gray upperparts; faint or no breastband.

Voice Song is a spaced series of clear notes on different pitches; call is a quiet "tuck."

Habitat Moist coniferous woods.
POPULATION: ⇑

Nesting Nest of twigs, moss, and occasionally mud, placed on horizontal branch of tree. Eggs: 2–5, light blue with brown spots; I: 14 days; F: unknown; B: unknown.

Attracting
May come to feeders for raisins, other fruit, or suet.

Female

Tip This bird looks a little like a robin, but note its orange wing bars and orange eyeline.

American Robin
Turdus migratorius 10"

I.D. **MALE:** Dark gray above; orange-brown below; white under tail; bright yellow bill.

Voice Song is a lively whistle, like "cheeryup cheerily"; calls include "teek" and "tuk tuk tuk."

Habitat Lives in many habitats, from woods to open lawns, from plains to the timberline of mountains. **POPULATION:** ↑

Nesting Nest of grass and mud, placed on limb of tree or building ledge. Eggs: 3–7, light blue; I: 12–14 days; F: 14–16 days; B: 2–3.

Female, p. 46
Male

Tip Most often seen running along lawns and tilting their heads to *see*, not hear, earthworms.

Attracting

May come to feeders for fruit such as raisins or berries.

Comes to birdbaths.

To attract, plant berry-producing shrubs and keep some areas of open lawn.

House Finch
Carpodacus mexicanus 5½"

I.D.
MALE: Red on head and upper breast; broad brown streaking on lower breast and sides.

Voice
Both male and female give a song that is a musical warble ending with a harsh downslurred "jeeer."

Habitat
Urban areas, suburbs, parks, canyons, semidry brush country.
POPULATION: ↑

Nesting
Nest of twigs and grasses, placed in shrub, vine, hanging planter, or birdhouse. Eggs: 2–6, bluish white with speckles; I: 12–16 days; F: 11–19 days; B: 1–3.

Female, p. 26

Male

 Tip **Common at feeders; often build their nests in hanging outdoor planters.**

Attracting

Eats a variety of seeds, especially sunflower and thistle.

Hole: 1⅜–2 in. dia. and 5–7 in. above floor
Floor: 4 x 4 in.

Comes to birdbaths to drink and bathe.

17

Purple Finch

Carpodacus purpureus 6"

I.D.
MALE: Upperparts, breast, and sides raspberry red; head uniformly red; little or no brown streaking on breast or sides.

Voice
Song is an extended warble; call while in flight is a short "pik."

Habitat
Mixed woods, coniferous forests, suburban yards. **POPULATION:** ↓

Nesting
Nest of twigs, grasses and rootlets, placed in tree. Eggs: 3–6, light blue-green with dark marks; I: 13 days; F: 14 days; B: 1–2.

Attracting
Attracted to sunflower, thistle, and millet seed, either scattered on the ground or in aboveground feeders.

Female, p. 27

Male

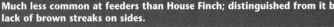
Tip Much less common at feeders than House Finch; distinguished from it by lack of brown streaks on sides.

Rufous Hummingbird
Selasphorus rufus 3¹/₂"

I.D.
MALE: All orange-brown except for orange-red iridescent throat and white collar.

Voice
Series of "chup" calls; male can create wing whistle, especially during displays.

Habitat
Woods edges, thickets, parks, gardens, mountain meadows.
POPULATION: ⇓

Nesting
Nest of downy fibers and moss held together with spider silk, placed on limb of tree or shrub. Eggs: 2, white; I: 12–14 days; F: 20 days; B: 1–2.

Attracting
Comes to hummingbird feeders.

Male

Female, p. 71

Tip The most aggressive of our hummingbirds, defending small feeding territories on its migration stops.

19

Common Yellowthroat
Geothlypis trichas 5"

I.D. **FEMALE:** Yellow throat and breast; whitish eye-ring; brown wash on forehead, back, and wings.

Voice Call is a sharp "tchet."

Habitat Dense brushy habitats near wet areas; also drier habitats with dense understory. **POPULATION:** ↓

Nesting Cuplike nest of grasses, leaves, and hair, placed in shrubbery. Eggs: 3–4, creamy white with brown marks; I: 12 days; F: 8–9 days; B: 1–2.

Male, p. 5

Female

Tip If you get near their nest, the birds will approach and give their "tchet" call.

Attracting
Planting shrubs near a lake or pond may attract them to nest.

House Wren

Troglodytes aedon 5"

I.D. A small bird with short tail often cocked up; upperparts grayish brown; underparts grayish white; some buffy barring on sides.

Voice Song is a bubbling warble lasting 2–3 seconds, often repeated.

Habitat Woods edges in rural or suburban areas; also mountain forests, clearings. POPULATION: ⇑

Nesting Nest of short twigs lined with hair and rootlets, placed in any natural or human-made cavity, including birdhouse. Eggs: 5–6, white with brown marks; I: 12–15 days; F: 16–17 days; B: 1–2.

Tip Male builds nest foundations in several birdhouses; female selects one and adds final lining.

Attracting

Hole: 1–1½" in. dia. and 6–7" in. above floor
Floor: 4 x 4 in.

21

Bewick's Wren
Thryomanes bewickii 5 1/2"

I.D.
A sleek wren with a white eyebrow; long tail marked with black and white underneath; underparts pale gray.

Voice
Song is a complex jumble of thin notes and trills; call is a "chip."

Habitat
Thickets, brush, and open woodlands in rural or suburban areas.
POPULATION: ↓

Nesting
Nest of twigs, hair, leaves, and grass lined with feathers, placed in cavity, such as mailbox, fence post, hole in wall, or birdhouse. Eggs: 4–11, white with dark spots; I: 14 days; F: 14 days; B: 1 or possibly more.

Attracting

Hole: 1 1/4–1 1/2 in. dia. and 6–7 in. above floor
Floor: 4 x 4 in.

Tip Often flicks its long tail from side to side, revealing the tail's white outer tips.

Lazuli Bunting

Passerina amoena 5¹/₂"

I.D.

FEMALE: Grayish brown above; light below with buffy wash on breast; 2 faint wing bars; light bluish cast to wings, tail, and rump.

Voice

Call is a short "pit."

Habitat

Shrubs and low trees in open areas, often near water.
POPULATION: ↑

Nesting

Nest of dried grass and weeds lined with horsehair and fine grass, placed in thicket, shrub, or small tree. Eggs: 3–5, light bluish white; I: 12 days; F: 10–15 days; B: 2–3.

Female

Male, p. 62

Tip Look for this bird on or near the ground as it searches for seeds and insects to eat.

Cliff Swallow

Hirundo pyrrhonota 6"

I.D. Buffy rump; whitish forehead; dark reddish-brown throat. Tip of tail is square and not forked.

Voice An extended harsh twittering is given by the male; both sexes give a "churr" call and a nasal "nyew" call, which is used during alarm.

Habitat Open areas near cliffs, bridges, outbuildings. POPULATION: ↑

Nesting Colonial. Nest is a spherical cavity with a narrow entrance tunnel, built of mud pellets mixed with a little grass and lined with feathers. Nests are sometimes built on cliffs, but usually under bridges, in culverts, and on buildings. Eggs: 2–5, white with brown blotches; I: 12–15 days; F: 24 days; B: 1–3.

Tip Cliff Swallows sometimes nest in very large colonies; look for their buffy rumps when they fly.

Pine Siskin
Carduelis pinus 5"

I.D. Small brown-streaked bird with varying amounts of yellow showing on wings and base of tail; bill is fairly long and sharply pointed.

Voice Calls include a repeated "swee-yeet" and a distinctive, buzzy, ascending "zreeeee."

Habitat Coniferous or mixed woods, shrub thickets, suburban yards. POPULATION: ↓

Nesting Nest of grasses, twigs, and rootlets, placed in tree. Eggs: 1–5, light blue-green with dark marks; I: 13 days; F: 14–15 days; B: 1–2.

Tip Seen most often in winter at feeders, often in the company of goldfinches.

Attracting

Comes to hanging feeders with thistle, hulled or black oil sunflower seed. Will also feed on seed scattered on ground.

House Finch

Carpodacus mexicanus 5½"

I.D. FEMALE: Uniformly finely streaked brown head; broad brown streaking on breast and belly.

Voice Both male and female give a song that is a musical warble ending with a harsh downslurred "jeeer."

Habitat Urban areas, suburbs, parks, canyons, semidry brush country. POPULATION: ↑

Nesting Nest of twigs and grasses, placed in shrub, vine, hanging planter, or birdhouse. Eggs: 2–6, bluish white with speckles; I: 12–16 days; F: 11–19 days; B: 1–3.

Male, p. 17

Female

 Tip Originally from West, expanding range in East; often build nests in hanging outdoor planters.

Attracting

Eats a variety of seeds, especially sunflower and thistle.

Hole: 1³⁄₈–2 in. dia. and 5–7 in. above floor
Floor: 4 x 4 in.

Comes to birdbaths to drink and bathe.

Purple Finch
Carpodacus purpureus 6"

I.D.
FEMALE: Well-defined pattern on face of a broad white eyebrow, brown eyeline, and white cheek. Broad, blurry, brown streaking on breast and belly.

Voice
Call while in flight is a short "pik."

Habitat
Mixed woods, coniferous forests, suburban yards. **POPULATION:** ↓

Nesting
Nest of twigs, grasses, and rootlets, placed in tree. Eggs: 3–6, light blue-green with dark marks; I: 13 days; F: 14 days; B: 1–2.

Attracting

Attracted to sunflower, thistle, and millet seed, either scattered on the ground or in above-ground feeders.

Male, p. 18

Female

Tip Much less common at feeders than the similar-looking female House Finch, which lacks white eyebrow.

House Sparrow
Passer domesticus 6"

I.D.

MALE: Black bib; gray crown and cheek; rich brown back and nape. In fall, black bib is hidden by gray tips of fresh feathers. **FEMALE:** Grayish-brown breast; brown crown; buffy eyebrow; yellow bill.

Voice

Calls include a "chirup chireep chirup."

Habitat

Urban areas and parks; also farmland where livestock is present. **POPULATION:** ⇓

Nesting

Messy nest of string, grass, and cloth, placed in crevice or birdhouse. Eggs: 3–7, white, or light blue with dark marks; I: 10–14 days; F: 14–17 days; B: 2–3.

Attracting
Eats all types of seed from a variety of feeders.

Female

Male

Male, fall

Tip **Also called English Sparrow because it was introduced from England; most common sparrowlike bird in cities.**

Aggressive at nest sites and may kill or evict native species from birdhouses. Cannot enter nest holes smaller than 1 1/8 in.

Dark-eyed Junco
Junco hyemalis 6"

I.D. Dark hood; brown back; white belly and pale bill. Male has black hood; female has brown hood.

Voice Calls include "tsip" and "zeet"; song is a short trill.

Habitat Summers in woods, bogs, mountains above tree level; winters in woods edges, brush, suburban yards. POPULATION: ↓

Nesting Cuplike nest of grasses and moss, placed in depression in ground near tall vegetation. Eggs: 3–6, gray or pale bluish with dark blotches; I: 12–13 days; F: 9–13 days; B: 1–2.

Attracting

Prefers seed scattered on the ground, such as millet, cracked corn, or hulled sunflower.

Tip One of the most common winter visitors at suburban and rural feeders; usually in flocks.

Uses brush piles for daytime safety and nighttime roosting.

Chipping Sparrow
Spizella passerina 5 1/2"

I.D.

SUMMER: Clear gray breast; bright reddish-brown crown; thin black eyeline. **WINTER:** Head is buffier and less distinctly colored; brown crown has fine black streaks; eyeline is faint.

Voice

Song is a continuous rapid trill, 2–3 seconds long.

Habitat

Grassy areas, open woods, lawns, parks. **POPULATION:** ↑

Nesting

Cuplike nest of grasses and sometimes horsehair, placed on branch of tree. Eggs: 3–4, pale blue with dark blotches; I: 11–12 days; F: 7–10 days; B: 2.

Attracting

Comes to feeders for mixed seed scattered on the ground or for hulled sunflower seed in hanging feeders.

Tip Common in suburban yards, nesting in evergreen foundation plantings.

Planting dense evergreens in your yard is a good way to attract nesting Chipping Sparrows.

30

Song Sparrow
Me *Melospiza melodia* 6"

I.D.
Brown-streaked whitish breast with a dark central dot; long tail rounded at tip; gray eyebrow; heavy brown marks off base of bill.

Voice
Song is repeated notes followed by a rich and varied warble, like "maids, maids, maids, put on your tea kettle ettle ettle."

Habitat
Dense shrubs at edge of fields, lawns, streams. **POPULATION:** ↓

Nesting
Cuplike nest of grasses, placed on ground or in shrub. Eggs: 3–5, greenish white with dark marks; I: 12–13 days; F: 10 days; B: 2–3.

Tip When disturbed, it often flies to the top of a nearby shrub and gives its "tchup" call.

Attracting

Comes to feeders where seed such as cracked corn, millet, or hulled sunflower is scattered on ground.

Lark Sparrow
Chondestes grammacus 6½"

I.D.
Striking red-brown cheek patch and crown stripes; clear gray breast with central dot. **IN FLIGHT:** Its long tail shows white spots at the two outer corners.

Voice
Complex song of trills, clear notes, and buzzes; call is a sharp "tsip," sometimes given in a series.

Habitat
Open woods, farmland, roadsides, open residential areas. **POPULATION:** ⇓

Nesting
Cuplike nest of grass lined with rootlets, placed on ground. Eggs: 4–5, white with dark marks; I: 11–12 days; F: 9–10 days; B: 1.

Tip Look for the bold face pattern of this fairly common roadside bird; often in flocks.

White-crowned Sparrow

Zonotrichia leucophrys 7"

I.D.

ADULT: Head boldly streaked with black and white; pink-orange bill; gray face and nape; clear gray breast. IMMATURE: Head similar to adult, but colors of streaks reddish brown and grayish brown instead of black and white. Imm. plumage kept until spring.

Voice

Song varies; often whistled notes and a trill; call is a sharp "pink."

Habitat

Lives in variety of habitats, including wet meadows, shrubby borders, woods, gardens, parks. POPULATION: ↓

Nesting

Nest of grass, twigs, and plant stems, placed on ground or in shrub. Eggs: 3–5, pale blue or green with darker spots; I: 11–15 days; F: 10 days; B: 1–4.

Immature

Adult

Tip This sparrow looks mostly gray except for the clean black-and-white stripes on its head.

Attracting

Comes to mixed seed scattered on the ground.

33

Golden-crowned Sparrow
Zonotrichia atricapilla 7"

I.D. **ADULT:** Black crown with a bold golden patch in the center; gray face; white eye-ring; clear gray breast. **IMMATURE:** Crown golden in front, brown in back; face and breast brownish. Imm. plumage kept until spring.

Voice Song is 3–4 downslurred whistles, like the phrase "oh dear me."

Habitat Summers in mountain thickets and shrubs; winters in brushy areas. **POPULATION:** ↓

Nesting Nest of grass, ferns, and sticks, placed on ground or bank in shallow depression. Eggs: 3–5, creamy or light blue; I: unknown; F: unknown; B: 1 or more.

Adult

Immature

Tip You are most likely to see this bird in winter, looking for seeds on the ground at your feeder. Look for its gold crown.

Attracting

Comes to mixed seed scattered on the ground or placed on a platform above the ground.

Cedar Waxwing
Bombycilla cedrorum 7"

I.D. Sleek and crested; brownish above; yellow on belly; red dots on tips of wings; yellow tip to tail.

Voice Most Cedar Waxwing calls are very high-pitched whistles; flight call sounds like "seeee seeee."

Habitat Open rural or suburban areas. **POPULATION:** ⇑

Nesting Nest of grasses, twigs, and moss, placed in fork or branch of tree. Eggs: 2–6, pale with dark marks; I: 12–16 days; F: 14–18 days; B: 1–2.

Attracting
Attract Cedar Waxwings by planting trees and shrubs that produce berries or small fruits, which they eat.

Tip Almost always in flocks and often seen flying about trees and shrubs with berries.

35

Brown-headed Cowbird
Molothrus ater 7"

I.D.
FEMALE: Grayish brown overall with very little distinct marking; dark gray conical bill; faint streaking on breast. Often seen with more easily recognized male.

Voice
Calls include a high-pitched "pseeseee" and a chattering "ch'ch'ch'ch."

Habitat
Pastures, woods edges, lawns, forest clearings. **POPULATION:** ↓

Nesting
A female cowbird lays her eggs in the nests of other species, which then raise her young. Eggs: Usually only 1 per host nest, white with dark marks; I: 10–13 days; F: 9–11 days; B: unknown.

Attracting
Eats seed mixes scattered on the ground. Since cowbirds are parasitic on other birds, most people try to discourage them at feeders.

Male, p. 79
Female
Tip Females are often seen in the company of several males that are displaying as they compete for her.

Black-headed Grosbeak
Pheucticus melanocephalus 8"

I.D. **FEMALE:** Large bill; buffy eyebrow; light streaking on buffy breast; 2 white wing bars. **IN FLIGHT:** Shows yellow "armpits."

Voice Call is a squeaky "eek."

Habitat Deciduous forests, thickets, pine woodlands. **POPULATION:** ↑

Nesting Nest of twigs, rootlets, and flower heads, placed in fork of tree or shrub. Eggs: 2–5, bluish white or greenish white with brown spots; I: 12–13 days; F: 11–12 days; B: 1 or possibly more.

Attracting
Comes to feeders for fruit or sunflower and mixed seed.

Male, p. 12

Female

Tip Listening for the squeaky call is a good way to find and identify the female.

Cactus Wren

Campylorhynchus brunneicapillus

8"

I.D. Our largest wren. Dark crown; wide white eyebrow; heavily spotted breast; barred wings. Long tail barred black and white underneath.

Voice Song is a loud "cha cha cha cha" or "choo choo choo choo."

Habitat Deserts and semideserts with cactus, such as prickly pear, cholla, saguaro. POPULATION: ↓

Nesting Large football-shaped nest of plant stems and grass has side entrance leading through small passage to inner chamber. Nest is placed in cactus or other thorny plant. Eggs: 3–7, pinkish white with dark marks; I: 16 days; F: 19–23 days; B: 2–3.

 Tip Easy to find in the desert because of its constant calling and endless curiosity.

Attracting

May visit bird feeders for bread, seeds, or pieces of fruit.

Horned Lark
Eremophila alpestris 8"

I.D. Distinctive black facial marks—black forehead with black "horns" (more prominent on males); black bib. Other areas on face, throat, and belly vary from whitish to deep yellow.

Voice Song is a light twittering, given during display flight; call "tsee-titi" or "zeet."

Habitat Open ground with low vegetation. POPULATION: ↓

Nesting Nest a depression in ground lined with grasses, placed near grass clump or clod of manure. Eggs: 3–5, gray, sometimes spotted with brown; I: 11 days; F: 9–12 days; B: 1–3.

Tip Look for Horned Larks on the ground in open fields or other open areas with sparse vegetation.

Spotted Towhee
Pipilo maculatus 8"

I.D.

Voice

Habitat

Nesting

FEMALE: Brown hood, back, and wings contrast with reddish-brown flanks and white belly; white spotting on wings.

Calls are "chewink" or "chweee."

Open woods with shrub understory. **POPULATION:** ↑

Nest of leaves, strips of bark, and grass, placed on or near ground in scratched depression under brush. Eggs: 2–6, creamy with brown spots; I: 12–13 days; F: 10–12 days; B: 1–3.

Attracting

Comes to feeders for mixed seed scattered on ground.

Female

Male, p. 13

Tip Listen for the rustling sound it makes in underbrush as it jumps backward to pull away leaves and search for seeds.

California Towhee
Pipilo crissalis 9"

I.D. Uniformly dark grayish brown overall; long tail with reddish brown under base; buffy throat bordered by short streaks; no central breast dot or reddish-brown crown.

Voice Song consists of accelerating "chink" notes; call is "chink."

Habitat Scrub and suburban yards.
POPULATION: ⇓

Nesting Nest of small twigs, grass, plant stems, and rootlets, placed on ground or in low bush. Eggs: 2–6, light blue with dark marks; I: 11 days; F: 8 days; B: 2–3.

 Tip May be quite tame and visit bird feeders or come to picnic tables for bits of food.

Attracting
 Comes to bird feeders for mixed seed scattered on the ground.

Comes to birdbaths for drinking and bathing.

Red-winged Blackbird

Agelaius phoeniceus 8½"

Male, p. 82

Female

I.D.

FEMALE: Brown above; heavily streaked brown below; sharp-pointed bill; buffy-to-whitish eyebrow.

Voice

A loud "ch'ch'ch'chee chee chee"; also "check" and "tseeert."

Habitat

Marshes and wet meadows.
POPULATION: ↓

Nesting

Nest of reeds and grasses attached to standing grasses or shrub. Eggs: 3–5, pale greenish blue with dark marks; I: 11 days; F: 11 days; B: 2–3.

Tip Look for females among grasses and cattails, where they build the nests and raise the young.

Attracting

Comes to feeders, especially in late summer, and eats seed scattered on the ground. Favors cracked corn and hulled or black oil sunflower seed.

Brewer's Blackbird

Euphagus cyanocephalus 9"

I.D. FEMALE: All grayish brown; dark eye.

Voice Call is "chick."

Habitat Wet meadows, river borders, cultivated areas, parks, urban areas, roadsides. POPULATION: ↓

Nesting Nest of twigs, grass, and mud, placed on or just above ground in low vegetation. Eggs: 3–7, pale gray with dark marks; I: 12–14 days; F: 13–14 days; B: 1–2.

Attracting
Comes to feeders with mixed seed scattered on the ground.

Female

Male, p. 83

Tip This bird is about the size and proportions of a robin, but all grayish brown.

Yellow-headed Blackbird

Xanthocephalus xanthocephalus
9 1/2"

I.D. **FEMALE:** Grayish brown overall except for yellow chin and breast; white streaks on upper belly.

Voice Call is a low "krrt."

Habitat Summers in marshes; winters in grain fields. **POPULATION:** ⇑

Nesting Nest of reeds and grass lined with softer materials, placed low in vegetation above water. Eggs: 3–5, pale greenish with dark marks; I: 11–13 days; F: 9–12 days; B: 2.

Male, p. 11

Female

Tip In summer, look for it in marshes; in winter, look for it among large flocks of other blackbirds, starlings, and cowbirds.

American Kestrel
Falco sparverius 9"

I.D. Small brownish falcon; two black sideburns on each side of face.
MALE: Has blue-gray wings.
FEMALE: Has reddish-brown wings.

Voice Common call is a series of sharp staccato notes like "klee klee klee klee" directed at intruders around nest.

Habitat A wide variety of open habitats, including urban areas.
POPULATION: ↑

Nesting Nests in a natural cavity or birdhouse. Eggs: 3–7, pinkish with dark marks; I: 29–31 days; F: 29–31 days; B: 1.

Attracting

Kestrels can be attracted with nest boxes placed 15–30 ft. high on a pole or tree in open areas.

Female

Male

Tip Often seen perched atop trees along highways, where they hunt for voles.

Hole: 3 in. dia. and 10–12 in. above floor
Floor: 8 x 8 in.

American Robin
Turdus migratorius 10"

I.D.

FEMALE: Brown above; pale reddish brown below; white under tail; bright yellow bill.

Voice

Calls include "teek" and "tuk tuk tuk."

Habitat

Lives in many habitats, from woods to open lawns, from plains to the timberline of mountains.
POPULATION: ↑

Nesting

Nest of grass and mud, placed on limb of tree or building ledge. Eggs: 3–7, light blue; I: 12–14 days; F: 14–16 days; B: 2–3.

Male, p. 16

Female

Tip Most often seen running along lawns and tilting their heads to *see*, not hear, earthworms.

Attracting

May come to feeders for fruit, such as raisins or berries.

Comes to birdbaths.

To attract, plant berry-producing shrubs and keep some areas of open lawn.

Killdeer
Charadrius vociferus 10"

I.D. Dark brown above, whitish below; 2 dark neck-rings.

Voice Many varied calls. The most common is a repeated 2-part "killdeah," sounding much like the bird's name.

Habitat Open ground with gravel or short grass; suburban or rural.
POPULATION: ↓

Nesting Nest is a scrape in the ground with a few pebbles added. Eggs: 3–4, pale brown with darker marks; I: 24–28 days; F: 25 days; B: 1–2.

Tip Famous for their "broken-wing display," in which they look injured in order to distract predators from their nest or young.

Attracting
May nest in gravel areas or sparse lawns. If Killdeers nest in your area, try to keep dogs and cats away from their nest, which is placed on the ground.

California Quail
Callipepla californica 10"

I.D. Small chickenlike bird; black plume on forehead; scaled appearance to belly. MALE: Black chin. FEMALE: Light chin.

Voice Call is a 3-note "chi-ca-go"; lower pitched than similar call of Gambel's Quail.

Habitat Open woodlands or shrubby areas, parks, suburbs; usually near water. POPULATION: ↓

Nesting Nest lined with grasses and dead leaves, placed in scraped depression near log or rock. Eggs: 12–16, creamy white with dark marks; I: 18–23 days; F: 10 days; B: 1–2.

Attracting
Comes to seed and grain placed on the ground.

Female   Male

Tip Listen for the loud call of this quail to know when it is in the area.

Gambel's Quail
Callipepla gambelii 11"

I.D.
Small chickenlike bird; black plume on forehead; reddish-brown sides; unscaled belly. **MALE:** Black chin. **FEMALE:** Light chin.

Voice
Most common call is a 4-note "chi-ca-go-go."

Habitat
Arid scrubby areas, also streamside woodlands. **POPULATION:** ↓

Nesting
Nest lined with twigs, grass, and leaves, placed in scraped depression at base of vegetation. Eggs: 9–14, buff with dark marks; I: 21–24 days; F: 10 days; B: 1–2.

Attracting

Comes to seed scattered on the ground. Feeds primarily in morning and late afternoon.

Female
Male

Tip Only quail in Arizona and New Mexico with a "topknot." Usually seen running about in small groups.

49

Curve-billed Thrasher
Toxostoma curvirostre 10½"

I.D. Long noticeably downcurved bill; large, blurry, rounded spotting on upper breast; orangish eye.

Voice Song is whistled phrases; call is an emphatic "whit-weet."

Habitat Semidesert scrub, suburban parks and yards. POPULATION: ⇓

Nesting Nest of twigs, grass, and leaves, placed in cactus, thorny bush, or small tree. Eggs: 1–5, light greenish blue with brown spots; I: 12–15 days; F: 12–18 days; B: 2–3.

Attracting
May come to bird feeders for fruit.

Tip You can most easily find this bird by listening for its loudly whistled "whit-weet" call.

California Thrasher

Toxostoma redivivum 12"

I.D. Dark brown above; long strongly downcurved bill; buffy belly and undertail; dark eye.

Voice Song is repeated phrases mimicking other birds; call is "chuck."

Habitat Chaparral.
POPULATION: ⇓

Nesting Nest of twigs, plant stems, and grasses, placed in dense bush or small tree. Eggs: 2–4, light blue with light brown spots; I: 14 days; F: 12–14 days; B: 2.

Attracting
Comes to bird feeders for sunflower seed, mixed seed, cracked corn, suet, and fruit such as raisins.

Tip Look for this bird running on the ground through brush with its tail cocked up.

Mourning Dove
Zenaida macroura 12"

I.D. A sleek, gray-brown, pigeonlike bird; long pointed tail; large black dots on wings.

Voice Common call heard during spring and summer is a cooing that sounds like "ooahoo oo oo oo."

Habitat Can be found in almost any habitat. POPULATION: ↓

Nesting Nest is a loose platform of twigs, placed in tree. Eggs: 2, white; I: 14–15 days; F: 12–14 days; B: 2–3.

Attracting

Prefers seed scattered on the ground, such as white millet, sunflower seed, and cracked corn.

Comes to birdbaths, where it can suck up water through its bill, unlike other birds that need to tilt their heads back to swallow.

Tip During cooing call, given by unmated males, they puff out their throat feathers and bob their tails.

Northern Flicker
Colaptes auratus 13"

I.D. Red patch on back of neck; wide black necklace; whitish or buffy breast with black spots; brown-and-black-barred back and wings. IN FLIGHT: Note white rump and yellow underwings.

Voice A loud "kekekekeke" heard in early spring and a softer "woika-woikawoika" during courtship.

Habitat Parks, suburbs, farmland, woodlands. POPULATION: ⇓

Nesting Excavates nest cavity in dead tree, post, or cactus; may also use birdhouse. Eggs: 7–9, white; I: 11–12 days; F: 14–21 days; B: 1–2.

Attracting

Comes to suet at feeders; may also eat some seeds, such as hulled sunflower.

Male

Female

Tip Flickers are often seen feeding on the ground, looking for one of their favorite foods — ants.

Hole: 2–3 in. dia. and 10–20 in. above floor
Floor: 7 x 7 in.

Wood Duck
Aix sponsa 18"

I.D. **FEMALE:** Grayish brown with a darker crown and broad white eye-ring that tapers to a point at the back.

Voice Call in flight is a distinctive "oo-eeek oo-eeek" given only by the female.

Habitat Wooded swamps and rivers. **POPULATION:** ⇑

Nesting Nest of wood chips and down, placed in natural tree cavity or birdhouse, over ground or over water. Eggs: 10–15, dull white; I: 27–30 days; F: 56–70 days; B: 1–2.

Attracting

A large birdhouse mounted on a pole a few feet above water can attract these ducks.

Hole: 3–4 in. dia. and 16–18 in. above floor
Floor: 10 x 10 in.

Male, p. 74

Female

Tip Female often seen taking care of the young by herself in summer.

Cooper's Hawk
Accipiter cooperii 16"

I.D. **ADULT:** Blue-gray above, lighter below with reddish-brown barring. **IMMATURE:** Brown above with brown streaking below.

Voice A rapid series of high "kek kek kek kek" notes most often given near nest.

Habitat Mixed forests and open woodlands. **POPULATION:** ↑

Nesting Nest is a platform of sticks lined with bark, placed in tree. Eggs: 3–6, pale blue-green with dark marks; I: 32–36 days; F: 27–34 days; B: 1.

Attracting
Cooper's Hawks sometimes catch birds at feeders; brush or cover near feeders provides safety for other birds.

Immature

Adult

Tip A small long-tailed hawk, usually first seen chasing small birds at feeders.

Red-tailed Hawk
Buteo jamaicensis 19"

I.D. White chest; dark head; variable band of streaking across breast; tail reddish on adult when seen from above as the bird tilts and soars.

Voice A loud downslurred scream, like "tseeeaarr," sometimes given while soaring overhead.

Habitat Variety of open habitats, especially farmland, roadside grasslands. **POPULATION:** ⇑

Nesting Nest is a platform of twigs lined with bark and greenery, placed in tree. Eggs: 1–5, bluish white with dark marks; I: 28–35 days; F: 44–46 days; B: 1.

Tip Most common hawk seen perched in trees along highways, where it hunts voles in the grass.

I.D.

Barn Owl
Tyto alba 18"

Slim long-legged owl; large, white, heart-shaped facial disk; dark eyes; breast white to buffy and sparsely spotted.

Voice

Mostly harsh hissing or screeching sounds; some metallic clicks.

Habitat

Open farmland, grasslands, deserts, suburbs. **POPULATION:** ↓

Nesting

Nests in barns and other old buildings, tree hollows, church steeples, old burrows of wood-chucks, and holes in banks. Will use human-made nest boxes. Eggs: 4–7, white; I: 32–34 days; F: 45–58 days; B: 1–2.

Attracting

Hole: 6–8 in. dia. and 4 in. above floor
Floor: 16 in. wide, 22 in. deep

Tip Our only owl with a heart-shaped face; can catch mice in total darkness, just by hearing them.

Great Horned Owl
Bubo virginianus 22"

I.D. Very large owl; widely spaced ear tufts; yellow eyes; white throat that sometimes continues in a thin V down the chest.

Voice Four to six deep resonant hoots, given in various rhythms. Sometimes like "hoohoohoo hoohoo hoo."

Habitat Extremely varied; woods, suburbs, even deserts. POPULATION: ↑

Nesting Uses old nest of hawk or crow and adds feathers to the lining from its own breast. Eggs: 1–4, white; I: 28–30 days; F: 35 days; B: 1.

Tip Crows often mob this owl, and their drawn-out caws are often a clue to the owl's presence.

Mallard
Anas platyrhynchos 24"

Male, p. 75

Female

Male, p. 75

I.D. FEMALE: A brown-streaked duck; orange bill broadly marked with black in the center; whitish tail feathers; dark blue feathers on wings sometimes visible.

Voice Female gives a series of descending quacks; also a soft "quege-gege."

Habitat Lakes, rivers, ocean bays, parks. POPULATION: ↑

Nesting Nest of reeds and grasses lined with down, placed on ground near water. Eggs: 8–10, pale greenish white; I: 26–30 days; F: 50–60 days; B: 1.

Tip Only females can make the quacking sound; male calls are a short whistle and a "rhaeb."

Attracting
Attracted to cracked corn scattered on the ground; will not come to feeders unless they are near water where ducks normally live.

Small ponds may attract them for feeding and/or nesting.

Canada Goose
Branta canadensis 36"

I.D. A large common goose seen in park ponds or grazing on lawns. Brownish gray overall; black head and neck; white chin.

Voice Male gives a low "ahonk" call; female gives a higher "hink" call, often alternating in a duet with the male.

Habitat Summers on lakes and marshes; winters on lakes, bays, fields, parks. **POPULATION:** ⇑

Nesting Nest of sticks, moss, and grass lined with down, placed on ground at edge of water or on grass hummock. Eggs: 4–7, white; I: 28 days; F: 2–3 weeks; B: 1.

Attracting
Eats cracked corn but in general should not be fed because it gets too used to humans and becomes a problem in public areas, fouling lawns and small ponds with droppings.

Tip Common goose in parks. In long-distance flights, flies in V formations or diagonal lines.

Brown Pelican
Pelecanus occidentalis 45"

I.D. Large coastal bird; large dark bill; dark throat pouch; gray-brown body. Nape is dark brown in breeding adults; whitish in non-breeding adults. IMMATURE: All dark grayish brown.

Voice Usually quiet when away from breeding grounds.

Habitat Coastal. POPULATION: ⇑

Nesting Nests colonially on coastal islands. Nest is a rim of soil and debris on ground, or of sticks and grass in a tree. Eggs: 2–4, white; I: 28–30 days; F: 71–88 days; B: 1.

Adult, breeding

Immature

Tip Dives from air to catch fish in its pouch; small flocks seen gliding low over water in line formations.

Attracting
Attracted to fish in coastal bays and often roosts during the day in tall trees near these sites.

Lazuli Bunting

Passerina amoena 5¹/₂"

I.D.
MALE: Bright sky-blue head and back; reddish breast; white belly; 2 white wing bars.

Voice
Song is a rapid jumble of whistled notes; call is a short "pit."

Habitat
Shrubs and low trees in open areas, often near water.
POPULATION: ↑

Nesting
Nest of dried grass and weeds lined with horsehair and fine grass, placed in thicket, shrub, or small tree. Eggs: 3–5, light bluish white; I: 12 days; F: 10–15 days; B: 2–3.

Female, p. 23

Male

Tip Look for this bird on or near the ground as it searches for seeds and insects to eat.

Tree Swallow
Tachycineta bicolor 6"

I.D. Iridescent blue above; pure white below. Females in their first 2 years are mostly brown above and white below.

Voice Common call is a loud "cheedeep cheedeep."

Habitat Open areas near woods and water. **POPULATION:** ⇑

Nesting Nest of grasses lined with feathers, placed in old woodpecker hole or birdhouse. Eggs: 5–6, white; I: 14–15 days; F: 21 days; B: 1–2.

Tip **Generally seen in more rural areas, soaring through the air as they catch insects.**

Attracting

Tree Swallows readily accept birdhouses on poles out in the open.

Hole: 1¹/₂ in. dia. and 6–7 in. above floor
Floor: 5 x 5 in.

Barn Swallow
Hirundo rustica 7"

I.D. Upperparts iridescent blue; belly buff; throat reddish brown; tail forked.

Voice Both sexes give a song of continuous twittering interspersed by grating sounds; during feeding or alarm they call "chitchit."

Habitat Open country near barns or open outbuildings, bridges, culverts.
POPULATION: ↑

Nesting Nest is deep bowl of mud pellets and grass lined with feathers, placed on beam or ledge in barn, under bridge, or in large culvert. Eggs: 2–7, white with reddish-brown speckles; I: 14–16 days; F: 18–23 days; B: 1–3.

Attracting
By creating ledges in an open outbuilding or leaving a window or door to a barn open, you may attract nesting Barn Swallows.

Tip Usually seen flying, it is best recognized by its long forked tail and reddish-brown throat.

Western Bluebird
Sialia mexicana 6¹/₂"

I.D. **MALE:** Deep purplish blue on head, throat, wings, and tail; brick-red on breast; usually shows chestnut patch on back. **FEMALE:** Gray throat; buffy breast; grayish-blue head and back; light blue wings and tail; white eye-ring.

Voice Song a mixture of "cheer," "chup," and "chur chur"; call is "chweeer."

Habitat Forest edges, open woods, lowlands in winter. **POPULATION:** ↓

Nesting Nest of weed stems and grass lined with hair and often feathers, placed in natural cavity or birdhouse. Eggs: 5–8, pale blue; I: 13–17 days; F: 19–22 days; B: 2–3.

Attracting
Eats berries, raisins, and mealworms at feeders.

Male

Female

Tip The male Western Bluebird is the only bluebird with a blue chin and a red breast.

Hole: 1⁹/₁₆ in. dia. and 6–7 in. above floor. Floor: 5 x 5 in.

Comes to birdbaths for drinking and bathing.

Mountain Bluebird
Sialia currocoides 6¹/₂"

I.D. **MALE:** Sky-blue above; lighter blue below. **FEMALE:** Uniformly pale grayish-brown body; wings and tail sky-blue (color best seen when the bird flies); white eye-ring.

Voice Song is short sequences of a variety of "chur's" and rattles; call is "churchur."

Habitat Summers in mountain meadows, rangeland, sagebrush; winters in lowlands, including desert.
POPULATION: ⇑

Nesting Nest of grasses, twigs, and pine needles, placed in birdhouse, natural cavity, or building. Eggs: 4–8, pale blue; I: 12–16 days; F: 19–23 days; B: 2.

Attracting

May visit bird feeders for berries or raisins in winter.

Female

Male

Tip This bluebird often hovers several feet above the ground as it searches for insects to eat.

Hole: 1⁹/₁₆ in. dia. and 6–7 in. above floor
Floor: 5¹/₂ x 5¹/₂ in.

Steller's Jay
Cyanocitta stelleri 13"

I.D.
Prominent crest; brownish-black head, breast, and back grading to a deep blue on wings, belly, rump, and tail; small white marks on forehead and around eye vary in prominence between individuals.

Voice
Most common call is a repeated "shaack shaack shaack."

Habitat
Mostly mountain coniferous forests. POPULATION: ↑

Nesting
Bulky nest of twigs, leaves, and mud, placed in shrub or tree. Eggs: 2–6, blue or pale green marked with brown; I: 16 days; F: 18 days; B: 1.

Attracting
Eats table scraps at picnic sites. At feeders eats sunflower seed and suet.

Tip These noisy birds often visit picnic sites or campsites in small groups, where they look for handouts.

Comes to birdbaths for drinking and bathing.

Western Scrub-Jay
Aphelocoma californica 12"

I.D.
Blue head, wings, and tail; no crest; throat streaked gray and white bordered by a bluish necklace; thin white eyebrow; grayish back.

Voice
Calls are varied and include a chattering "kaykaykaykay."

Habitat
Variety of habitats, including brushy open country, desert scrub, orchards, canyons.
POPULATION: ⇑

Nesting
Nest of twigs, grass, and rootlets, placed in shrub or bush. Eggs: 2–6, pale green or gray with reddish-brown marks; I: 16–19 days; F: 18 days; B: 1–2.

Attracting
Comes to bird feeders, where it eats a wide variety of seeds as well as suet.

Tip **Distinguished from other jays by its lack of a crest and its gray-streaked throat; often tame at picnic areas.**

Comes to birdbaths for drinking and bathing.

68

Allen's Hummingbird
Selasphorus sasin 3½"

 I.D.

MALE: Orange-brown on tail and sides; green on back and crown; red iridescent throat. **FEMALE:** Green upperparts; orange-brown tail and sides; white throat and central belly; iridescent dots on throat. Female cannot be distinguished in the field from female Rufous Hummingbird.

 Voice

Series of "chup" calls; male can create wing whistle, especially during displays.

 Habitat

Woods, thickets, gardens, parks.
POPULATION: ↓

 Nesting

Nest of downy fibers and moss held together with spider silk, placed on vine or shrub limb. Eggs: 2, white; I: 15–17 days; F: 22–25 days; B: 1–2.

Male

Female

 Tip This species migrates north along the coast as early as January.

Attracting
Comes to hummingbird feeders.

Black-chinned Hummingbird

Archilochus alexandri 3½"

I.D.

MALE: Black chin bordered by violet (violet may appear black in some lights); chest and central belly white; back and sides green. **FEMALE:** Green above; white below; throat clear to evenly and lightly streaked; repeatedly spreads and flips tail while hovering at feeder.

Voice

Call is a descending "tyew."

Habitat

Dry lowlands and foothills. **POPULATION:** ↑

Nesting

Nest of plant down, feathers, lichens bound together with spider silk, placed on branch of tree or shrub. Eggs: 1–3, white; I: 13–16 days; F: 21 days; B: 1–2.

Male

Female

Tip Violet chin of male and tail-bobbing of female in flight are best clues to this species.

Attracting
Comes to hummingbird feeders.

Rufous Hummingbird

Selasphorus rufus 3¹/₂"

I.D.

FEMALE: Green upperparts; orange-brown tail and sides; white throat and central belly; iridescent dots on throat. Female cannot be distinguished in the field from female Allen's Hummingbird.

Voice

Series of "chup" calls.

Habitat

Woods edges, thickets, parks, gardens, mountain meadows.
POPULATION: ⇓

Nesting

Nest of downy fibers and moss held together with spider silk, placed on limb of tree or shrub. Eggs: 2, white; I: 12–14 days; F: 20 days; B: 1–2.

Attracting

Comes to hummingbird feeders.

Female

Male, p. 19

Tip The most aggressive of our hummingbirds, defending small feeding territories on its migration stops.

71

Anna's Hummingbird

Calypte anna 4"

I.D.

MALE: Bright rose iridescence on throat and crown; green back and sides; white chest and central belly. **FEMALE:** Green upperparts; light underparts; red spotting on throat that may form a small patch.

Voice

Complex song is a series of squeaky phrases; call is "chip."

Habitat

Open woods, shrubs, gardens, parks. **POPULATION:** ↓

Nesting

Nest of downy plant fibers, decorated with lichens, held together with spider silk; placed in a variety of locations, often near houses. Eggs: 2, white; I: 14–19 days; F: 18–23 days; B: 1–2.

Male

Female

Tip The only hummingbird regularly seen in winter along the West Coast; common in California gardens.

Attracting
Comes to hummingbird feeders.

Broad-tailed Hummingbird

Selasphorus platycerus 4"

I.D.

MALE: Upperparts green; throat iridescent rose-red (may appear black); breast and central belly whitish. **FEMALE:** Upperparts green; underparts whitish; pale buffy flanks; rufous at base of outer tail feathers.

Voice

Variety of chips and twitters.

Habitat

Open mountain woodlands and meadows. **POPULATION:** ↑

Nesting

Nest of downy materials covered with bits of bark and lichens held together with spider silk, placed on horizontal limb. Eggs: 2, white; I: 16–17 days; F: 18–23 days; B: 1–2.

Attracting
Comes to hummingbird feeders.

Male

Female

Tip Listen for the high-pitched buzz of male's wings when he is flying nearby.

Wood Duck
Aix sponsa 18"

I.D.
MALE: Distinctive colorful head with iridescent green. White throat, partial neck-ring, and chinstrap.

Voice
Male gives high whistle; female gives distinctive "oo-eeek oo-eeek" call in flight.

Habitat
Wooded swamps and rivers.
POPULATION: ⇑

Nesting
Nest of wood chips and down, placed in natural tree cavity or birdhouse, over ground or over water. Eggs: 10–15, dull white; I: 27–30 days; F: 56–70 days; B: 1–2.

Female, p. 54

Male

Tip Look for males gathering together in fall to do courtship displays that include flicking their chins up or to the side and raising wings and tails.

Attracting

A large birdhouse mounted on a pole a few feet above water can attract these ducks.

Hole: 3–4 in. dia. and 16–18 in. above floor
Floor: 10 x 10 in.

74

Mallard
Anas platyrhynchos 24"

I.D.

MALE: Iridescent green head; yellow bill; chestnut breast; white neck-ring may be hidden.

Voice

Male does not quack but gives a short whistle and a drawn-out "rhaeb" or short "rheb rheb" call.

Habitat

Lakes, rivers, ocean bays, parks.
POPULATION: ↑

Nesting

Nest of reeds and grasses lined with down, placed on ground near water. Eggs: 8–10, pale greenish white; I: 26–30 days; F: 50–60 days; B: 1.

Female, p. 59

Male

Tip Watch for males doing courtship displays in fall. They include the whistle call and fast swimming with head low.

Attracting

Attracted to cracked corn scattered on the ground; will not come to feeders unless they are near water where ducks normally live.

Small ponds may attract them for feeding and/or nesting.

I.D.
White overall; short, stocky, yellow-orange bill. Breeding adult has buffy-orange plumes on its head, back, and breast.

Voice
Gives a "kok" call when alarmed.

Habitat
Open dry areas, lawns, fields, pastures with livestock.
POPULATION: ⇑

Nesting
Nests with other herons in colonies. Nest of sticks, twigs, and reeds, placed in shrub or tree. Eggs: 2–6, bluish white; I: 21–24 days; F: 30 days; B: 1.

Tip A common small heron, often seen feeding along roads or in cattle fields.

Snowy Egret
Egretta thula 24"

I.D. White body; black bill; black legs with bright yellow feet (its "galoshes"). During breeding, the feet turn orange or red.

Voice During aggressive encounters with other herons, it gives a harsh "gaah" call.

Habitat Coastal areas, marshes, river valleys, lake edges. **POPULATION:** ⇑

Nesting Nests in large colonies or singly. Nest of sticks and twigs in a platform, placed on ground or in tree or shrub. Eggs: 3–5, pale bluish green; I: 20–29 days; F: 30 days; B: 1.

Tip Look for its yellow "galoshes" and black bill. May aggressively defend nest and feeding areas.

77

Great Egret
Ardea alba 39"

I.D. Large all-white heron; long yellow bill; legs and feet black. In the breeding season, adults grow long white plumes on their backs.

Voice Call is a deep rattlelike croak.

Habitat Marshes, swamps, seashores, lake margins. **POPULATION:** ⇑

Nesting Nests in colonies with other herons, ibises, and cormorants or singly. Nest is a flimsy platform of sticks, twigs, and reeds, placed in tree or shrub. Eggs: 1–6, pale bluish green; I: 23–26 days; F: 42–49 days; B: 1.

Tip Feeds in water or on land by walking slowly with head forward and then striking prey.

Brown-headed Cowbird

Molothrus ater 7"

I.D.

MALE: Glossy black body; dark brown head; dark gray conical bill.

Voice

Song is a liquid "bublucomsee"; calls include a high-pitched "pseeseee" and a chattering "ch'ch'ch'ch."

Habitat

Pastures, woods edges, urban lawns, forest clearings.
POPULATION: ↓

Nesting

A female cowbird lays her eggs in the nests of other species, which then raise her young. Eggs: Usually only 1 per host nest, white with dark marks; I: 10–13 days; F: 9–11 days; B: unknown.

Female, p. 36

Male

Tip Usually seen in small groups, feeding on grassy areas in summer; seen in large flocks in fall and winter.

Attracting

Eats seed scattered on the ground. Since cow- birds are parasitic on other birds, most people try to discourage them at feeders.

Phainopepla

Phainopepla nitens 7¹/₂"

I.D.

MALE: Glossy black; crest; red eye; long tail. **IN FLIGHT:** Note white patches on outer wings.

Voice

Song is a short warble; call is a low "wurp."

Habitat

Desert washes, oak woods. **POPULATION:** ⇑

Nesting

Nest of twigs, grass, flowers, and leaves bound with spiderweb, placed in fork of tree. Eggs: 2–4, grayish white with dark spots; I: 14–16 days; F: 19–20 days; B: 1–3.

Female, p. 108

Male

Tip Look for its white wing patches as it flies into the air to catch insects.

European Starling
Sturnus vulgaris 8"

Winter

Summer

I.D.

SUMMER: A common city bird. Glossy purple-black overall; long yellow bill. Juveniles, which form large flocks in late summer, are brown and gradually change to black. **WINTER:** Black body speckled overall with white and gold; black bill. White and gold spots wear off by spring.

Voice

Song is a stream of squeals, squawks, and imitations of other birds' calls.

Habitat

Cities and suburbs. **POPULATION:** ↓

Nesting

Nest of grass, feathers, and flowers, in tree hole, birdhouse, or building crevice. Eggs: 2–8, light blue with dark marks; I: 12–14 days; F: 18–21 days; B: 1–3.

Tip Look for starlings perched near building nooks or tree holes, where they nest.

Attracting
At feeders eats suet and a variety of seeds.

Starlings, an introduced species, aggressively compete with native birds for nest holes. A birdhouse entrance hole of 1½ in. or smaller keeps them out.

Red-winged Blackbird

Agelaius phoeniceus 8½"

I.D.

MALE: All black with a red shoulder patch, which is bordered by yellow; the shoulder patch can be hidden.

Voice

Song is a loud "okaleee"; calls include "check" and "tseeert."

Habitat

Marshes and wet meadows.
POPULATION: ↓

Nesting

Nest of reeds and grasses attached to standing grass or shrub. Eggs: 3–5, pale greenish blue with dark marks; I: 11 days; F: 11 days; B: 2–3.

Attracting

Comes to feeders, especially in late summer, and eats seed scattered on the ground. Favors cracked corn and hulled sunflower seed, but also eats other types of mixed seed.

Female, p. 42

Male

Tip Look for males perched atop shrubs or cattails in marshes, singing and spreading their wings

I.D.

Brewer's Blackbird
Euphagus cyanocephalus 9"

MALE: Black with purplish gloss on head and greenish gloss on body; pale yellow eye. May have brownish-gray edges to body feathers in fall.

Voice

Song is a squeaky "kasqueek"; call is a "chick."

Habitat

Wet meadows, river borders, cultivated areas, parks, urban areas, roadsides. **POPULATION:** ↓

Nesting

Nest of twigs, grass, and mud, placed on or just above ground in low vegetation. Eggs: 3–7, pale gray with dark marks; I: 12–14 days; F: 13–14 days; B: 1–2.

Attracting

Comes to feeders with mixed seed scattered on the ground.

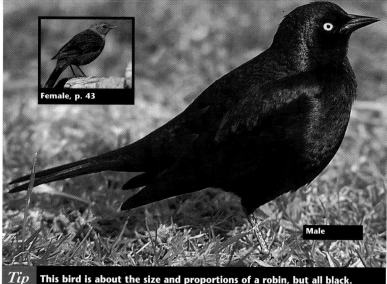

Female, p. 43

Male

Tip This bird is about the size and proportions of a robin, but all black.

83

Common Grackle
Quiscalus quiscula 12"

I.D. Black with iridescence on head, back, and belly; yellow eye. Female has shorter tail and less iridescence than male.

Voice Song is a short series of harsh sounds ending in a squeak, like "grideleeek"; calls include a "chaack" and "chaaah."

Habitat Open areas with some trees; city parks, urban yards, farmland. POPULATION: ↓

Nesting Nest of grass and mud, placed in shrub or tree. Eggs: 4–7, pale greenish brown with dark marks; I: 13–14 days; F: 12–16 days; B: 1.

Attracting
Attracted to sunflower seed and seed mixes scattered on the ground or on trays.

Tip **A common bird, often seen near water. Male flies with tail folded lengthwise during breeding.**

Comes to birdbaths for drinking and bathing.

American Crow

Corvus brachyrhynchos 18"

I.D. The familiar, very large, all-black bird with a large black bill.

Voice Varied types of caws, from short to long and descending.

Habitat Seen in just about all habitats.
POPULATION: ↑

Nesting Nest of twigs and sticks lined with bark and grass, placed in tree. Eggs: 4–5, bluish green with brown marks; I: 18 days; F: 28–35 days; B: 1–2.

Attracting

Comes to all kinds of seed at feeders; will eat suet if it can get it and is attracted to food scraps.

Tip **In fall and winter afternoons, crows fly in large numbers to nightly roosts.**

Turkey Vulture
Cathartes aura 26"

I.D. Very large; black with a small, featherless, red head; trailing half of wings silvery. When soaring, its wings are held in a V and it often tilts side to side.

Voice Vultures are silent except at the nest, where they may give grunts and hisses.

Habitat Open country and dumps, occasionally roost in urban areas. POPULATION: ↑

Nesting Nest is a scrape on bare ground, in cave, stump, cliff ledge, or old building. Eggs: 1–3, dull white; I: 38–41 days; F: 70–80 days; B: 1.

Tip They are most often seen soaring lazily along ridges or over fields, looking for carrion to eat.

Double-crested Cormorant
Phalacrocorax auritus 33"

I.D. Large; long neck and long bill; all black with a broad orange throat pouch beneath its bill. **IMMATURE:** In their first year, young cormorants are dark brown with a light brown throat and belly.

Voice Usually quiet away from nesting areas.

Habitat Coasts, inland rivers, and lakes. **POPULATION:** ⇑

Nesting Nests colonially. Platform nest of sticks and seaweed, placed in tree or on ground. Eggs: 2–7, pale blue; I: 24–29 days; F: 35–42 days; B: 1.

Adult
Immature

Tip Look for cormorants perched near water on rocks or dead branches, often holding wings out to dry.

Downy Woodpecker
Picoides pubescens 6"

I.D.

FEMALE: White spots on black wings; white belly and back; no red on back of head. Distinguished from similar Hairy Woodpecker by bill, which is about half as long as its head.

Voice

A high-pitched "teek" call and a call that sounds like the whinny of a miniature horse.

Habitat

Woods, farmland, suburbs.
POPULATION: ↑

Nesting

Excavates a nest cavity in dead wood. Eggs: 4–5, white; I: 12 days; F: 21 days; B: 1–2.

Attracting

Especially attracted to suet feeders but may also feed on hulled sunflower seed.

Male, p. 92

Female

Tip Seen hitching up tree trunks or along branches. May drum on resonant surfaces in spring as part of courtship.

Nuttall's Woodpecker
Picoides nuttallii 7"

I.D.

FEMALE: No red on head; black-and-white-barred back; white face and underparts; black eye-stripe is much wider than the black line off the base of the bill, and the two connect behind the cheek.

Voice

Calls include a 2-syllable "pitik" and a high-pitched whinny. Drumming is 1–2 seconds of rapid even taps.

Habitat

Shrublands, streamsides, oak woods. **POPULATION:** ↑

Nesting

Excavates nest cavity in dead wood, often willow, cottonwood, or oak. Eggs: 3–6, white; I: 14 days; F: 29 days; B: 1.

Attracting
Comes to suet feeders.

Female

Male, p. 93

Tip Distinguish it from the similar Downy Woodpecker by its barred rather than white back.

Black Phoebe
Sayornis nigricans 7"

I.D.
All black except for its white belly.

Voice
Song is an ascending then descending "peeyee yeewee"; call is a short "chirp."

Habitat
Wooded streams and canyons, farms and suburbs near water.
POPULATION: ⇑

Nesting
Nest is a cup made of mud mixed with hair and grass, stuck to vertical surface with some overhanging protection, such as cliff, wooden or concrete wall, or bridge. Eggs: 4–5, white; I: 15–18 days; F: 14–21 days; B: 2.

Tip **Repeatedly bobs tail when perched. Almost always found near water.**

Black-billed Magpie
Pica pica 20"

I.D. Body boldly marked with black and white; long tail; black bill. Wings and tail are iridescent, sometimes looking greenish.

Voice Alarm call is a rapid series of "chak" notes; also gives an ascending "maaag."

Habitat Open areas with trees and shrubs; farmlands, gardens, parks.
POPULATION: ↓

Nesting Nests alone or in loose colony. Large domed nest of thorny twigs has a side entrance and inner cup of mud, placed in tree or shrub. Eggs: 2–9, blue-green with brown speckles; I: 14–23 days; F: 10 days; B: 1.

 Tip **May mob crows to make them drop food items; uses communal roosts all year.**

Attracting
 Eats a variety of foods at feeders, including sunflower seed and cracked corn.

Downy Woodpecker
Picoides pubescens 6"

Female, p. 88

Male

I.D.

MALE: White spots on black wings; white belly and back; red on back of head. Distinguished from similar Hairy Woodpecker by its bill, which is about half as long as its head.

Voice

A high-pitched "teek" call and a call that sounds like the whinny of a miniature horse.

Habitat

Woods, farmland, suburbs.
POPULATION: ↑

Nesting

Excavates a nest cavity in dead wood. Eggs: 4–5, white; I: 12 days; F: 21 days; B: 1–2.

Tip Usually seen hitching up tree trunks. May drum on resonant surfaces in spring as part of courtship.

Attracting

Especially attracted to suet feeders but may also feed on hulled sunflower seed.

Nuttall's Woodpecker
Picoides nuttallii 7"

I.D.

MALE: Red on back of head; black-and-white-barred back; white face and underparts; black eye-stripe is much wider than the black line off the base of the bill, and the two connect behind the cheek.

Male

Female, p. 89

Voice

Calls include a 2-syllable "pitik" and a high-pitched whinny. Drumming is 1–2 seconds of rapid even taps.

Habitat

Shrublands, streamsides, oak woods. **POPULATION:** ↑

Tip Distinguish it from the similar Downy Woodpecker by its barred rather than white back.

Nesting

Excavates nest cavity in dead wood, often willow, cottonwood, or oak. Eggs: 3–6, white; I: 14 days; F: 29 days; B: 1.

Acorn Woodpecker
Melanerpes formicivorus 8"

I.D. Clear black back; red on crown; white eye surrounded by black; white forehead and cheek. **IN FLIGHT:** Note white rump and white patch near tip of wing. **MALE:** Red crown touches white forehead. **FEMALE:** Red on back half of crown separated from white forehead by black.

Voice Repeated "chacup chacup chacup."

Habitat Oak and pine woods, parks, suburbs. **POPULATION:** ↑

Nesting Nests in colonies. Excavates cavity in tree, usually oak. Eggs: 4–6, white; I: 14 days; F: 30–32 days; B: 2–3.

Attracting
Comes to feeders that have suet or seed.

Male

Female

Tip These noisy birds live in small groups and regularly store acorns in trees, telephone poles, and the sides of houses.

Bushtit
Psaltriparus minimus 3¹/₂"

I.D. Tiny and gray; tiny stubby beak; long tail. Coastal birds are light with a gray-brown cap; interior birds are dark with a brownish cheek; southwest males or juveniles may have a black cheek patch. **MALE:** Dark eyes. **FEMALE:** Light yellow eyes.

Voice Song is a high-pitched trill; calls include short "tseep" and "tsip."

Habitat Open woods, chaparral, suburbs, parks, gardens. **POPULATION:** ↓

Nesting Gourd-shaped nest of moss, rootlets, lichens, and feathers, attached by spider silk to twigs of tree or bush. Eggs: 5–7, white; I: 12 days; F: 14–15 days; B: 1–2.

Attracting

Comes to feeders for small seeds and hulled sunflower seed.

   Tip Through most of the year, these active little birds travel in flocks, giving constant soft calls.

Comes to birdbaths for drinking and bathing.

95

Golden-crowned Kinglet
Regulus satrapa 3¹/₂"

I.D.
Very small; black cap with yellow or yellow-and-orange crown; white eyebrow; dark eyeline. **MALE:** Yellow crown with orange center. **FEMALE:** Yellow crown.

Voice
Song is several high notes ending in a chatter; call is very high and like "tsee tsee tsee."

Habitat
Summers in coniferous woods; winters also in mixed and deciduous forests. **POPULATION:** ⇓

Nesting
Globular nest of moss, lichens, and spiderweb lined with rootlets and feathers, hung from tree branch. Eggs: 8–11, creamy white with dark marks; I: 14–15 days; F: 14–19 days; B: 2.

Tip Continually active as it feeds; often flicks its wings over its back. Usually found with chickadees and titmice. Note white eyebrow.

96

Ruby-crowned Kinglet
Regulus calendula 4¹/₂"

I.D. Very small; grayish green above; white eye-ring; no white eyebrow; 2 white wing bars. **MALE:** Red patch on crown, usually concealed. **FEMALE:** No patch on crown.

Voice Song is a series of descending high notes followed by 3-part phrases, like the words "see see see you you you look-at-me, look-at-me, look-at-me."

Tip Continually active as it feeds; often flicks its wings over its back. Usually found with chickadees and titmice. Note plain face.

Habitat Summers in coniferous woods; winters in woods and brushy edges. **POPULATION:** ↑

Nest of moss, twigs, and lichens, hung from branch of tree or shrub. Eggs: 5–11, creamy white with brown marks; I: 12 days; F: 12 days; B: 1 or more.

Nesting

American Goldfinch
Carduelis tristis 5"

I.D.

WINTER: Grayish or brownish with only a hint of yellow on face and body; black wings and tail.

Voice

Flight call is "perchicoree perchicoree."

Habitat

Open areas with shrubs and trees, farms, suburban yards, gardens. **POPULATION:** ↓

Nesting

Nest of weed bark fastened with caterpillar webbing, placed in shrub or tree. Eggs: 3–7, light blue; I: 12–14 days; F: 11–15 days; B: 1–2.

Attracting

Prefers thistle or hulled sunflower seed in hanging feeders.

Male, summer, p. 4

Winter

 Tip Can look like different birds in summer because they change from mostly grayish brown to yellow.

Comes to birdbaths for drinking and bathing.

Yellow-rumped Warbler
Dendroica coronata 5½"

I.D.
In all seasons, note yellow rump, yellow patches in front of each wing, and yellow throat. FALL: Brownish gray above with streaks on breast, sides, and back. SPRING: Female similar to fall but grayer. Male slate-gray above with yellow crown and black on breast.

Voice
Song is a 2-note trill; common call is a "check."

Habitat
Summers in coniferous or mixed forests. In fall, brushy thickets. POPULATION: ↑

Male, summer

Adult, winter

Tip Look for these birds in fall, for they are very common during their southward migration.

Nesting
Cuplike nest of twigs, grasses, and rootlets, placed in conifer. Eggs: 4–5, cream with brown marks; I: 12–13 days; F: 12–14 days; B: 2.

Attracting

May come to feeders for suet and fruit.

Black-capped Chickadee
Parus atricapillus 5"

I.D.
Black cap and bib; white cheek; gray back; variable buff on sides.

Voice
Two whistled notes, the 1st higher than the 2nd, like "feebee." Calls include "tseet" and "chickadeedeedee."

Habitat
Woods, farmland, suburbs.
POPULATION: ↓

Nesting
Nest in tree hole or birdhouse includes moss. Eggs: 6–8, white with speckles; I: 11–12 days; F: 15–17 days; B: 1–2.

 Tip In winter, chickadees stay in small flocks that defend a territory against other chickadees.

Attracting

Prefers sunflower seed and suet in aboveground feeders.

Hole: 1¹/₈–1¹/₂ in. dia. and 6–7 in. above floor
Floor: 4 x 4 in.

Comes to birdbaths for drinking and bathing.

Chestnut-backed Chickadee
Parus rufescens 5"

I.D. Dark gray cap; black bib; white cheek; rich reddish-brown back; flanks gray or reddish brown.

Voice Calls are a hoarse "chik-zee-zee" and a "chek chek." Has no whistled song.

Habitat Coniferous or mixed woods. POPULATION: ↓

Nesting Nest of moss, hair, and feathers, placed in natural or excavated tree cavity, or birdhouse. Eggs: 6–7, white with light reddish speckles; I: 11–12 days; F: 13–17 days; B: 1–2.

Attracting
Comes to feeders for sunflower seed and suet.

Tip Our most colorful chickadee and the most common in the Northwest.

 Hole: 1¹/₈–1¹/₂ in. dia. and 6–7 in. above floor. Floor: 4 x 4 in.

 Comes to birdbaths for drinking and bathing.

101

Mountain Chickadee

Parus gambeli 6"

I.D. Black cap and bib; white cheek; thin white line over eye; gray flanks.

Voice Song is 3–4 whistled notes, such as "feebee feebee" or "fee bee bay." Calls include a raspy "chickadeedeedee."

Habitat Open coniferous forests in mountains. POPULATION: ↑

Nesting Nest of wood chips, hair, and feathers, placed in natural or excavated cavity, or birdhouse. Eggs: 7–9, white; I: 14 days; F: 17–20 days; B: 1–2.

 Tip This is the most common chickadee of mountain areas; note its white eyebrow.

Attracting
Comes to feeders for sunflower seed and suet.

Hole: $1^1/_8$–$1^1/_2$ in. dia. and 6–7 in. above floor. Floor: 4 x 4 in.

 Comes to birdbaths for drinking and bathing.

Plain Titmouse

Parus inornatus 5¹/₂"

I.D.
Small; all plain gray; small crest.

Voice
Song is a whistled "teewee teewee teewee"; call is "tsika-deedee."

Habitat
Sparse pinyon-juniper and oak woodlands. POPULATION: ⇓

Nesting
Nest composed of moss, grass, fur, and feathers, placed in natural cavity, old woodpecker hole, or birdhouse. Eggs: 6–8, whitish, sometimes with small brown dots; I: 14–16 days; F: 16–21 days; B: 1–2.

 Tip Named for its plain color; male feeds female in spring as part of courtship.

Attracting
Comes to feeders and prefers sunflower seed.

Hole: 1³/₈–1¹/₂ in. dia. and 6–7 in. above floor
Floor: 4 x 4 in.

Comes to birdbaths for drinking and bathing.

Red-breasted Nuthatch

Sitta canadensis 4¹/₂"

Male

I.D.
Dark crown and nape; white face; black eye-stripe; rust-colored breast. **MALE:** Black cap and richly colored underparts. **FEMALE:** Gray cap and lightly colored underparts.

Voice
Common call is a nasal "nyeep nyeep nyeep."

Habitat
Coniferous woods.
POPULATION: ⇑

Nesting
Nest of rootlets, grass, and moss, placed in excavated hole, birdhouse, or natural cavity. Eggs: 5–7, white or slightly pink with brown spots; I: 12 days; F: 16–21 days; B: 1–2.

Tip **Nuthatches are our only birds that can climb headfirst down tree trunks. This species is seen mostly in winter.**

Attracting
Prefers sunflower seed and suet feeders.

Hole: 1¹/₈–1¹/₂ in. dia. and 6–7 in. above floor
Floor: 4 x 4 in.

White-breasted Nuthatch
Sitta carolinensis 6"

I.D. Dark crown and nape; white face; gray back. In general, the crown is black on males and gray on females.

Voice Common call is a nasal "ank," given singly when the birds are calmly feeding or in a rapid series when they are disturbed.

Habitat Woods. **POPULATION:** ⇑

Nesting Nest of twigs, bark, and fur, placed in natural cavity or birdhouse. Eggs: 3–10, white with dark marks; I: 12 days; F: 14 days; B: 1–2.

Attracting
Prefers sunflower seed and suet mixtures.

Tip Nuthatches are our only birds that can climb headfirst down tree trunks.

 Hole: 1¹/₈–1¹/₂ in. dia. and 6–7 in. above floor
Floor: 4 x 4 in.

105

Western Wood-Pewee
Contopus sordidulus 6"

I.D.
Grayish olive above; whitish or yellowish on belly; grayish chest; prominent peak at back of head; 2 whitish wing bars; upper bill black; lower bill usually has some orange at base.

Voice
Song is "fee-rrr-reet." Call is a buzzy descending "feeer."

Habitat
Open woods, streamside trees.
POPULATION: ↓

Nesting
Compact nest of plant fibers and downy materials, covered with lichens, placed on horizontal limb of tree. Eggs: 2–4, creamy white with darker marks at one end; I: 12–13 days; F: 14–18 days; B: 1.

Tip Perches upright; also flies out after insects and then returns to the same perch.

Wrentit
Chamaea fasciata 6"

I.D. Plain grayish-brown bird; long tail; pale eye; faint streaking on breast. Birds are more reddish in the North, more grayish in the South.

Voice Song is short whistled notes speeding up and ending in a descending trill; female version of song lacks trill; call is "churr."

Habitat Chaparral, tangled brush, or dense shrubs. **POPULATION:** ↓

Nesting Nest of spiderweb, bark, and grasses, placed in twigs of shrub. Eggs: 3–5, pale greenish blue; I: 15–16 days; F: 15–16 days; B: 1 or possibly more.

Tip This common bird often stays hidden in underbrush; listen for its song to know it is nearby.

Phainopepla
Phainopepla nitens 7½"

I.D.
FEMALE: Gray; crest; red eye; long tail. **IN FLIGHT:** Note white patches on outer wings.

Voice
Call is a low "wurp."

Habitat
Desert washes, oak woods. **POPULATION:** ⇑

Nesting
Nest of twigs, grass, flowers, and leaves bound with spiderweb, placed in fork of tree. Eggs: 2–4, grayish white with dark spots; I: 14–16 days; F: 19–20 days; B: 1–3.

Male, p. 80
Female

Tip Look for its white wing patches as it flies into the air to catch insects.

108

I.D.

SUMMER: Upper parts reddish to orange-brown with darker brown streaking; belly white; legs black. **WINTER:** Pale gray above; white below; black legs; straight relatively short (for a shorebird) bill; small black patch on shoulder sometimes visible.

Voice

Flight call is a quiet "kip."

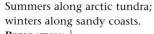

Habitat

Summers along arctic tundra; winters along sandy coasts. **POPULATION:** ↓

Nesting

Nest a scraped depression on dry tundra. Eggs: 4, olive-green with dark marks; I: 24–31 days; F: 17 days; B: 1–2.

Winter

Tip Most often seen on the beach in winter, barely avoiding the edges of the waves as it feeds.

Western Kingbird
Tyrannus verticalis 9"

I.D. Relatively short bill; head, throat, and upper breast light gray; belly bright yellow; square-tipped tail black with thin white edges, which are distinctive but sometimes hard to see.

Voice Call is "kit," sometimes extended to "kit kit kittledot."

Habitat Open areas with some trees or shrubs. POPULATION: ⇑

Nesting Bulky nest of twigs, plant stems, and rootlets, placed in tree. Eggs: 3–5, white with darker marks; I: 13–15 days; F: 16–18 days; B: 1 or possibly more.

Tip **Most widespread kingbird in West, often seen perched on telephone line or wire fence.**

Western Screech-Owl
Otus kennicottii 9"

I.D. Small owl with yellow eyes and "ear tufts" (actually just feathers on top of its head, which can be lowered and hidden); dark bill. There are 2 forms: a rare reddish form seen mostly in the Northwest; and a more common gray form seen in the rest of the range.

Voice A series of low-pitched whistles, starting slow and speeding up at the end.

Habitat Woods, swamps, deserts, parks, suburbs. POPULATION: ↓

Nesting Nests in tree cavity, saguaro cactus, old woodpecker hole, or birdhouse. Eggs: 2–5, white; I: 21–30 days; F: 28 days; B: 1.

 Tip Often seen peering out of nest hole during the day. May catch nighttime insects at streetlights.

Attracting
Hole: 3–4 in. dia. and 10–12 in. above floor
Floor: 8 x 8 in.

Northern Mockingbird
Mimus polyglottos 11"

I.D.
Grayish above; whitish below; long tail. IN FLIGHT: Note the bold white patches on its wings and white on its outer tail feathers.

Voice
Mimics other birds' songs and calls, repeating each 3 or more times.

Habitat
Open areas with shrubs; gardens, parks. POPULATION: ↓

Nesting
Nest of twigs and leaves, placed in shrub. Eggs: 2–6, blue-green with brown marks; I: 12–13 days; F: 10–13 days; B: 1–3.

Attracting
May come to feeders for fruits such as raisins.

Planting shrubs with berries may attract the birds to nest in them in spring and eat from them all winter.

Tip One of the few birds to sing in fall; may also sing on moonlit nights from spring through fall.

112

Pigeon (Rock Dove)
Columba livia 13"

I.D. The Pigeon is familiar to all. Due to breeding by humans, it can range in color from all white to all black, with just about anything in between.

Voice At nest sites, such as above air conditioners, you hear "k't'-cooo"; during courtship displays the male calls "oorook'tookoo."

Habitat Cities, parks, bridges, steep cliffs. POPULATION: ↑

Nesting Saucerlike nest of roots, stems, and leaves, placed on building ledge, rafter, or beam under bridge. Eggs: 1–2, white; I: 18 days; F: 25–29 days; B: 2–5.

Attracting
Covering ledges with screening can prevent nesting on houses.

Typical form

Variations

Tip Pigeons originally came from England, where they nest on steep cliffs; that is why they love tall buildings in cities.

Comes to feeders with mixed seed scattered on the ground.

113

Band-tailed Pigeon
Columba fasciata 14"

I.D. Dark gray wings and back; purplish head and breast; white band on back of neck with iridescence below it; bill yellow with black tip. **IN FLIGHT:** Note dark rump and wide light gray band at tip of tail.

Voice Low-pitched "oohooo."

Habitat Dry pine forests inland; oak forests along coast; may be seen in parks and gardens.
POPULATION: ⇓

Nesting Nest is a flimsy platform of sticks and twigs lined with pine needles, placed in fork or on horizontal branch of tree. Eggs: 1–2, white; I: 18–20 days; F: 25–27 days; B: 2–3.

Attracting

Comes to ground or platform feeders with sunflower or mixed seed.

Tip You can tell a flock of Band-tailed Pigeons from regular Pigeons because they all look alike; Pigeons vary.

Drinks at birdbaths.

114

Greater Yellowlegs
Tringa melanoleuca 14"

I.D. Long yellow-to-orange legs; long, thin, dark bill; whitish marks on dark upperparts; lighter underparts. The Lesser Yellowlegs is very similar but smaller and with a proportionately shorter bill.

Voice Call is a descending series of 3–4 notes, like "tew tew tew." Lesser Yellowlegs has a 2-note call, "tew tew."

Habitat Summers on subarctic forest bogs; winters on coastal marshes, beaches. POPULATION: ↑

Nesting Nest is a depression in the ground. Eggs: 4, buff with dark marks; I: 23 days; F: 18–20 days; B: 1.

Greater

Lesser

Tip Seen mostly from late summer through winter. Look for their long bright yellow legs.

115

Willet
Catoptrophorus semipalmatus 15"

I.D. Long, straight, rather heavy bill; long grayish legs. **WINTER:** Plain gray-brown above; whitish below. **SUMMER:** Brown streaking on head and neck; brown barring on breast. **IN FLIGHT:** Note distinctive bold white wing-stripe on black wing.

Voice Calls include a shrill "pill will willet" and a "kip kip kip."

Habitat Summers on coastal marshes in East and prairie marshes in West; winters on coastal marshes, beaches, mudflats. **POPULATION:** ↓

Nesting Nest a shallow scrape in ground lined with dry grass, placed in open area near water. Eggs: 4, olive with dark marks; I: 22–29 days; F: unknown; B: 1.

Winter

Winter

Summer

Tip Seen by most people in fall and winter along the coast, where it feeds on beaches and in mudflats.

116

California Gull
Larus californicus 19"

I.D.

ADULT: Greenish-yellow legs; black-and-red spot near tip of lower bill; dark eye; gray back. **IMMATURE—1ST YEAR:** Dark brown head and body; barring on wings and back; pink bill with well-defined dark tip; pink legs. Takes 4 years to reach adult plumage.

Voice

One common call is a soft "kow kow kow."

Habitat

Summers on lakes; winters along coast. **POPULATION:** ↓

Nesting

Colonial nester. Nest of weeds, grass, and trash bits, placed on ground. Eggs: 3, olive with dark marks; I: 23–27 days; F: unknown; B: 1.

Adult, summer

Adult, winter

Immature, 1st year

Tip Seen in summer breeding around lakes; especially common near Great Salt Lake.

Ring-billed Gull
Larus delawarensis 19"

I.D.

ADULT: Clear black ring just before tip of thin yellow bill; back and wings light gray. **IMMATURE—1ST YEAR:** Pale dark-tipped bill; gray back; light brown mottling on head and breast. Takes 3 years to reach adult plumage.

Voice

"Hyoh hyoh" and other calls.

Habitat

Coasts, lakes, dumps, fields.
POPULATION: ⇑

Nesting

Usually nests in colonies. Nest of grasses, pebbles, and sticks, placed on ground. Eggs: 3, light brown with dark marks; I: 21 days; F: unknown; B: 1.

Adult, winter

Immature, 1st year

Adult, summer

Tip **Gulls outside fast-food restaurants are almost always Ring-billed Gulls.**

118

Western Gull
Larus occidentalis 26"

I.D.

ADULT: Dark back and wings; white body; large yellow bill; pink legs. **IMMATURE—1ST YEAR:** Mottled grayish brown overall; all-black bill in winter has pale base following summer. Takes 4 years to reach adult plumage.

Voice

Low-pitched "cuk cuk cuk."

Habitat

Coastal.
POPULATION: ↓

Nesting

Colonial. Nest of grass, placed on ground or rocky ledge. Eggs: 3, olive with dark marks; I: 25–29 days; F: 40–50 days; B: 1.

Adult, winter
Adult, summer
Immature, 1st year

Tip **Only common dark-backed white-bodied gull in the West.**

Great Blue Heron

Ardea herodias 50"

I.D. Very tall; grayish-blue body; white head; black stripe over eye.

Voice When competing with other herons, it may give a guttural "frahnk" or short "rok-rok."

Habitat Marshes, swamps, river and lake edges, tidal flats, mangroves, other water areas. **POPULATION:** ⇑

Nesting Nests in small colonies or singly. Nest is a large platform of sticks lined with other vegetation, placed in dead tree, often over water. Eggs: 3–7, pale bluish green; I: 28 days; F: 55–60 days; B: 1.

Tip Our largest and most widespread heron, it is usually seen feeding; often mistaken for a crane.

THE**STOKES**GUIDES

STOKES FIELD GUIDES

Each with more than 900 full-color photographs—the easiest-to-use and most comprehensive field guides to North American birds

Stokes Field Guide to Birds: Eastern Region
0-316-81809-7

Stokes Field Guide to Birds: Western Region
0-316-81810-0

STOKES BEGINNER'S GUIDES

With full-color identification photographs—complete information on 100 common species

Stokes Beginner's Guide to Birds: Eastern Region
0-316-81811-9

Stokes Beginner's Guide to Birds: Western Region
0-316-81812-7

STOKES BACKYARD NATURE BOOKS

Illustrated guides to attracting and enjoying wildlife in your own yard—with full-color photographs throughout

Stokes Bird Feeder Book
0-316-81733-3

Stokes Bird Gardening Book
0-316-81836-4

Stokes Birdhouse Book
0-316-81714-7

Stokes Bluebird Book
0-316-81745-7

Stokes Butterfly Book
0-316-81780-5

Stokes Hummingbird Book
0-316-81715-5

Stokes Purple Martin Book
0-316-81702-3

Stokes Wildflower Book: East of the Rockies
0-316-81786-4

Stokes Wildflower Book: From the Rockies West
0-316-81801-1

STOKES NATURE GUIDES

Uniquely informative handbooks for observing plants and animal behavior in the wild

Stokes Guide to Amphibians and Reptiles
0-316-81713-9

Stokes Guide to Animal Tracking and Behavior
0-316-81734-1

Stokes Guide to Bird Behavior, Volume I
0-316-81725-2

Stokes Guide to Bird Behavior, Volume II
0-316-81729-5

Stokes Guide to Bird Behavior, Volume III
0-316-81717-1

Stokes Guide to Enjoying Wildflowers
0-316-81731-7

Stokes Guide to Nature in Winter
0-316-81723-6

Stokes Guide to Observing Insect Lives
0-316-81727-9

Published by
Little, Brown and Company

STOKES FIELD GUIDES TO BIRD SONGS

The best sound recordings of the birds of North America—available from Time Warner AudioBooks

Stokes Field Guide to Bird Songs: Eastern Region

3 CDs:
1-57042-483-7

3 cassettes:
1-57042-482-9